seasons of flowers

Design by Talmage McLaurin
Text by Dianne Noland

introduction

Flowers and foliages are the original harbingers of the seasons. More than anything else, the right flowers can create the perfect mood for a room, a dinner, a celebration. We all understand how the first bunch of daffodils can bring springtime to even the darkest winter day.

Although worldwide flower production has made many commercial varieties available on a year-round basis, most flowers are best appreciated during their natural blooming cycles. And that is the simple message of this book. For everything, there is a season.

The spectacular photographs used throughout this book all contain the floral designs of Talmage McLaurin, AIFD. Most were originally presented in the pages of Florists' Review magazine, where Talmage has reigned as creative director for over 10 years. His great artistic talent, refined good taste, and respect for nature's gifts are apparent in each image.

The text accompanying the photographs was written by Dianne Noland, instructor of horticulture at the University of Illinois. Over the years, Dianne has worked with our staff at Florists' Review on several projects. Her knowledge of floral products, accompanied by her precise use of the English language, makes her text a pleasure to read.

The concept of this book, as with any project from Florists' Review, is to increase your love and knowledge of flowers. Any season of the year.

Frances Dudley, publisher
Florists' Review Enterprises

forward

When I was a boy, I helped prepare flowers for funeral sprays and arranged holiday specials in our family flower shop. My mom patiently taught me the bread-and-butter of American floristry and the rules of classic design.

As my career developed, my design style became softer and more spontaneous. I now realize that this change was influenced by my grandmother, who would gather budding branches, daffodils, and wild hyacinths to create her own effortless arrangements, void of convention. I loved the way they showcased the flowers in a manner both pure and unaffected. The way I see flowers resulted from the blended visions of these two dear ladies.

My approach to floral design respects the tenets of the classic, yet it is not encumbered. Nature itself celebrates freedom, embraces the happenstance, and promotes individual expression. So do I.

Seasons of Flowers contains what I feel are the best images of my 10 years of work at *Florists' Review*. It's my hope that the flowers speak to you the way they did to me.

Talmage McLaurin is a vice president of *Florists' Review*, the floral industry's oldest and only independent magazine. He has been with the magazine for 10 years and is responsible for its creative endeavors. Talmage's work has been featured in several books including *Florists' Review's 101 How-to Favorites (2000)*, *World Floral Artist 2 (1999)*, *Florists' Review Weddings (1998)*, and *Florists' Review Christmas (1996)*. He was inducted into the American Institute of Floral Design in 1988 and has presented two National Symposium programs, one on wedding bouquets and the other on funeral tributes.

Dianne Noland, author, is a horticulture instructor at the University of Illinois and has served the floral and garden industries for more than 26 years as a horticulturist and educator. She has received numerous teaching awards, including her 1996 induction into the College of ACES Academy of Teaching Excellence. Mrs. Noland has co-authored 10 books, and in 1999, she took over as host of the PBS show *Illinois Gardener*.

spring

PHOTOGRAPHY BY STEPHEN SMITH

summer

autumn

PHOTOGRAPHY BY MARK ROBBINS

winter

PHOTOGRAPHY BY MARK ROBBINS

PHOTOGRAPHY BY MARK ROBBINS

spring
seasons of flowers

Spring is a season dominated by bulb flowers. In all shapes, sizes, and colors, bulb flowers are gorgeous when planted in pots or presented as cut flowers. Daffodils, tulips, hyacinths, grape hyacinths, and Irises are welcome and expected in spring bouquets.

Bulbs are not the only spring flowers available, however. Anemones, Freesias, snapdragons, sweet Williams, sweet peas, and stocks are also springtime favorites. Pastel colors like lavender, pale yellow, and pink are quite popular, particularly around Easter. But who can resist a pail full of lipstick-red spring tulips?

9

Above: A profusion of brightly colored tulips, Freesias, Ranunculuses, and amaryllises burst forth from a simple container, declaring the glorious arrival of spring. In hues from clear pink to fiery red, this gorgeous gathering of blossoms will chase the winter chills from any heart. **Design Tip:** Tying a haphazard raffia bow around the rim of the planter adds a casual, country flavor to this springy design.

Opposite page: A drop-in bouquet of pink tulips and white Freesias is accented by touches of fluffy pink feathers entwined among the flowers, which are arranged in clear glass to show off the smooth, clean stems and add more contrasting green color to the design. **Design Tip:** A simple addition, such as colored feathers on beading wire, can add a touch of whimsy to a simple arrangement, making it come alive.

Opposite page: Asymmetrically arranged in a contemporary container, this exquisite gathering of budding branches, blooming foliage, and colorful spring florals makes a wonderful accent to enliven the home. **Design Tip:** Use uniquely formed lines of branches and foliage to create an asymmetrical, free-form shape. Pull the abstract lines together with a vibrantly colored central mass, such as these Gerbera daisies, at the focal point.

Above: Accenting this casual arrangement of Anemones, miniature amaryllises, and drumstick Alliums is a contemporary "bow" of Allium stems and a quick-to-make wreath of heather. For efficiency, this arrangement is hand-tied and dropped into a plastic vase inside the terra-cotta pot. **Design Tip:** Add a unique accent to floral designs by saving a few smooth stems and tying them to the design with a pretty ribbon.

13

Opposite page: The combination of garden Irises, Alliums, foxtail lilies, larkspurs, lily grass, and coral bell foliage touch, rest, and support their companions in a tiny integrated garden. The vertical design allows the materials to interact, as if their tiny plot of growing space has forced them together. **Design Tip:** *Lily grass is often used as an airy, free-flowing accent. Try weaving it around other botanicals in a vertical arrangement for a textured, solid look.*

Below: An elegant silver mint julep glass graciously complements the small yet stunning blooms of these glorious grape hyacinths (Muscari). Filling a small container with an abundance of still-banded stems offers a full, added-value appearance, but you must loosen the ties to avoid a vase-life-reducing mold problem. **Design Tip:** *Take the flowers out of their bunch before arranging, and be sure that all of the flower heads are at the same height for maximum bloom visibility.*

Hyacinths offer a delightful fragrance and beautiful form in a spring bouquet. These lovely flowers have had a featured place in gardens and spring arrangements since the 17th century. The hyacinth, *Hyacinthus orientalis*, is native to the Mediterranean region from North Africa, Greece, Asia Minor, and Syria. The symbolic meaning of hyacinth in Victorian times was game, sport, or play.

spring hyacinths

The hyacinth is a dense oval raceme with numerous waxy, bell-shaped florets. The tips of each floret are pointed and flare open. Many cultivars are available. The fragrant flowers range in color from white, pink, blue, and purple as well as red, salmon, and yellow.

Hyacinths combine nicely with other bulb flowers, such as daffodils, *Irises*, and tulips, in spring vase arrangements or floral designs. Grouped hyacinths re-create the outdoors in garden-style designs. The fragrant raceme is a showy addition in contemporary designs, particularly botanical and parallel designs. The washed bulb and roots of the hyacinth can be placed within a contemporary design for eye-catching flair. In bridal bouquets, individual hyacinth florets can be wired and used as lovely fragrant accent flowers for the same look as *Stephanotis*. Wired chains of hyacinths add interest to a bride's or bridesmaid's bouquet.

Hyacinth plants add a fragrant, distinctive highlight in a planted garden arrangement with other blooming plants and arranged fresh flowers. The hyacinth pot should be placed in a liner to allow for its proper watering separately from the fresh flower arrangement.

Hyacinths are available throughout the spring months as a cut flower and a blooming plant. Since hyacinths will open fully from the bud stage, purchase flowers and plants with just a hint of color showing in the buds. Look for flowers with bright uniform color and numerous florets. Avoid plants with yellowed and misshapen leaves.

From the bud stage, hyacinths will provide four to eight days of enjoyment. Recut the stems and place them in cool water in a cool area. Keeping the vase or arrangement in a cool place will extend the lasting quality of these spring bulbs.

*At Left: Pretty pink hyacinths are "planted" in a chipwood box that was filled with raffia before the plastic liner was added. The raffia is cut to look like straw, and the fragrant flowers are arranged in foam to appear recently sprouted from their straw covering. **Design Tip:** Reinforce the casual, natural look of hyacinths by tucking raffia around the base of the flowers.*

*Opposite page: A casual gathering of hyacinths in a lovely pale lavender hue brings a breath of spring to interior environments. A rusted metal tub lends perfect contrast to the fresh blossoms and adds to the rustic charm of the design. **Design Tip:** A gathering of flowers doesn't have to look arranged to be effective. Try placing cut flowers in a container in the manner that they would grow, allowing a few leaves to protrude here and there.*

Above: As if growing toward the sunlight, the stems of these fragrant blooms arch gracefully from within the moss-topped pot in a realistic, garden-grown manner. **Design Tip:** To support the curved hyacinths in this vegetative design, use a brick of foam that fills two-thirds of the container, in both breadth and depth. Then, in an open area between the foam and the side of the pot, wedge the rubber-banded bunch of hyacinth stems.

Opposite page: The fragrance of this drop-in bouquet should invigorate the spirit, just as the rich accents of green ivy illuminate the muted tones of the Freesias and hyacinths. **Design Tip:** Use clippings from ivy plants as accents for spring floral designs. The cool green color and lovely shape of the leaves are welcome touches, particularly with soft-hued flowers.

Daffodils are a wonderful herald of spring! Their cheerful appearance gives hope that spring is here. The botanical name of daffodils or jonquils is *Narcissus*. In Greek mythology, Narcissus was a handsome youth who fell in love with his own reflection in a pool and was eventually transformed into the flower that bears his name. Not surprisingly, the symbolic meaning of *Narcissus* from Victorian times is egotism. Daffodil expresses regard, and jonquil says, "I desire a return of affection." Daffodils are native to Europe and North Africa.

Daffodils have six petals, which form a collar, or perianth, and other petals, which project forward, called the corona (also cup, crown, or trumpet). Flower colors are yellow, white, cream, and bicolors, including pink or orange cups. *Narcissi* are grouped into 12 divisions according to flower size and number of flowers. Daffodils may be single or double flowers and borne solitary or in small clusters. Many daffodils are lightly fragrant; paperwhite *Narcissi* are strongly fragrant.

spring daffodils

PHOTOGRAPHY BY STEPHEN SMITH

A sunny bouquet of daffodils can be designed as a vase arrangement for the longest lasting beauty. For a touch of fun and surprise, place lemons, to repeat the yellow colors, or hard-boiled eggs for a springy Easter theme, in the bottom of a clear vase, under water. Daffodils can also be arranged in a softer floral foam, developed specifically for spring flowers. An architectural grouping of *Narcissi* can be designed in floral foam in a sleek container with the foliage tucked into the narrow space between the foam and the inside edge of the container. To give support for weak daffodil stems, insert a chenille stem or thick wire into the cut end of each stem before inserting the stem into the floral foam.

Daffodils are available from December to April. Purchase *Narcissus* in the bud stage when just showing some color. The papery sheath covering the bud should be loosened and opening up. The buds and leaves should not appear shriveled or wilted.

Although daffodils are short-lived cut flowers, lasting three to six days, their fresh fragrance and crisp beauty are a pleasing reminder of spring. After purchasing daffodils, recut their stems and place them in a floral preservative solution, which limits bacterial growth. Keep *Narcissus* separate from other flowers for at least 24 hours after recutting the stems because they exude a gel-like substance that shortens the vase life of other flowers. Allow the stems to take up solution overnight.

Opposite page: A simple arrangement of daffodils in clear glass is accented by a few eggs submerged inside the vase. While pastel-dyed eggs would be pretty, the dye could discolor the water, so brown eggs, which echo the flowers' orange centers, are a natural choice for this creation. **Design Tip:** *When using clear glass vases, don't forget that there is plenty of design space below the water line. Look for interesting items to submerge under water.*

At right: Sunny yellow daffodils and crisp paperwhite Narcissi rise above simple clay pots in these easy-going, easy-to-prepare designs. Perfect for dressing up outdoor events, the casual gatherings will also brighten any room. However, the strong fragrance of paperwhites make them inappropriate for indoor dining. **Design Tip:** *Interesting mosses, pebbles, or pieces of driftwood can be tucked around flower stems to hide floral foam.*

Above: A glorious arrangement of daffodils, Ranunculuses, and orange chincherinchee (Ornithogalum dubium) is edged with Galax leaves and yellow feathers and placed casually in a ceramic pot. The off-center placement is intriguing for flower shop displays and home use. **Design Tip:** Florals don't have to fill up a container to be effective. Here, the bouquet is placed off center to show the visually pleasing hand-tied design.

Opposite page: An architecturally inspired column of cheery daffodils declares the arrival of spring in all its glory. These blossoms are arranged in floral foam, and the foliage accents are simply tucked in the narrow space between the pot and the foam. **Design Tip:** When choosing containers, take cues from flower color and shape. Here, tall flowers are regally displayed in a tall container, and the deep blue of the painted pot contrasts well with the orange flower centers.

Springtime is the time for tulips! Tulips have a distinctive flower shape that is universally linked to spring. The first tulips were found growing in Mediterranean Europe, northern regions of Africa, Turkey, Asia Minor, and China. The popularity of tulips is connected with the Dutch and other European plant breeders who have developed countless hybrids. Tulip is derived from the Turkish word *tulband*, meaning "turban." The botanical name is *Tulipa*. The meaning of tulip in the Victorian language of flowers is fame. Other meanings vary depending on the color. A red tulip indicates a declaration of love, a yellow tulip expresses hopeless love, and a tulip of several colors (bicolor) is for beautiful eyes.

Tulips are rounded flowers with colorful petals and sepals. Due to warmth and maturing, tulips open to form a bowl or cup shape. Most of the cut flower tulips are classified as single tulips. French tulips are single late types. Many other types are available, including double (peony-flowered), lily-flowered (pointed petals), parrot (ruffled and multicolored), and fringed-edge varieties.

A vase arrangement of all tulips is a classic, spring design. This style adapts to countless interiors and color schemes. Tulip stems will continue to elongate (one to two inches) as well as change shape and curve toward light in a design. Wiring is not helpful or recommended. A natural, loose style is more appropriate for the playful, changing tulip. Tulips combine beautifully with other spring flowers. A duet of tulips and Freesias is striking; a trio of tulips with *Irises* and flowering branches is springy and delightful. The light green leaves of tulips are a great addition to any design. Although longer lasting in vases, tulips can be designed in floral foam manufactured specifically for spring bulbs. One tip for floral foam designing is to allow the tulip stem to extend all the way through the foam to the bottom of the container for improved water uptake.

spring tulips

Tulips are commonly available from October to May. Select flowers that are still tightly closed but showing a hint of color. The stems should be straight and firm; the leaves should be a uniform green color and firm, not wilted.

The vase life of tulips is two to six days. Recut the stems, removing the white portion of the stem to insure better water uptake. Use a good floral preservative, carefully mixed into room temperature water, mainly to inhibit bacterial growth. To keep the stems straight before arranging, either leave the sleeves on the tulips or place the flowers in a tall, straight-sided container with a shallow level of solution (four to five inches). Store or display tulips in a cool area, avoiding sunlight and drafts.

*Opposite page: A near-complementary color harmony among the tulip blossoms makes for a bright and cheery composition in the chartreuse ceramic pot. For a natural, fluid, curving of the stems while still maintaining stability, these tulips are arranged in a thin layer of floral foam. **Design Tip:** Remember that because tulips will continue to elongate and reach toward light after they are arranged, it is best to design them in a natural, carefree way.*

*At Right: Classic spring tulips, in vibrant, eye-catching hues, take on a new look when they are surrounded by a "web" of lily grass (Liriope). The elegantly arching blades of grass offer an up-to-date foliage alternative. **Design Tip:** Tie a basic knot into the center of each blade of grass to form a "V." Tuck the two ends into the container to create the web effect.*

PHOTOGRAPHY BY STEPHEN SMITH

Above: Vibrant tulip blossoms, including red and bicolor 'Merry Widow,' make this a fabulous, eye-catching creation. The casual, carefree placements wonderfully suit these springtime beauties. **Design Tip:** Tuck in filler flowers, such as the heather and caspia shown here, around tulip stems, at the base of the design, to secure the loosely arranged flowers.

Opposite page: Pretty pastel tulips, gathered in a glorious cluster, unfailingly signal the arrival of spring. A smaller accessory arrangement, containing heather and delicate eggs, hint at more of spring's coming attractions. **Design Tip:** Curl the pliable heather stems around the inside of a clay pot to create the fluffy floral "nest" that beautifully supports the fragile egg accents.

Opposite page: An intriguing way to design spring's cut flowers is to "plant" them, or to arrange them so they appear to be potted. A profusion of blooms in a simple pot makes a wonderful decorative for any springtime occasion. **Design Tip:** *For a realistic potted presentation, cut stems to a uniform length, so most of the blooms will be on the same level. Top floral foam with moss for a natural-looking "ground cover," and consider incorporating elements such as pebbles and soil for added realism.*

Above: A simple white ceramic pot allows the brilliant colors of these tulips, as well as the vivid green foliage, to shine. In hues of yellow, pink, orange, red, and all shades in between, these gorgeous blooms welcome spring in a bright and festive way. **Design Tip:** *Along with traditional foliages, try some unusual varieties to give different looks. Here, ruffly ornamental kale adds welcome contrast in both color and texture.*

Above: A monochromatic collection of ruffle-edged tulips seems to embody all that is spring. Very little foliage is used to allow the peach color to make a bold statement. **Design Tip:** With monochromatic arrangements, the container's color can be an important contrast. Here, a lighter hue is selected to blend with the color of the flowers rather than contrast it.

Opposite page: Tulips in glorious red and yellow hues are elegantly showcased in a stately, fan-shaped antique silver vase. To accommodate continued growth, the tulips are allowed to gracefully bend over the container's edge. **Design Tip:** Work with the shape of the container, not against it. This tulip arrangement takes its cues from the fan shape of the vase.

An iris looks like a graceful dancer. That beauty inspired its naming after the Greek goddess of the rainbow, and its shape inspired the French to create the fleur-de-lis. Wisdom is its symbolic meaning in the language of flowers. The *Iris* or Dutch iris, so popular for floral designs, is native to Spain, Portugal, and northern regions of Africa.

Irises are grown from either bulbs or rhizomes. Those popular for floral designing year-round are the bulbous iris or Dutch iris (*Iris* hybrids). The garden types, grown from rhizomes, flower in spring gardens. Dutch irises are available in purple, blue, yellow, white, and bicolors. Each flower has three inner petals, called standards, and three outer petals, called falls, which fall down and away from the center. The falls usually have a small area of contrasting color. *Iris* leaves are medium green and very linear.

spring
irises

Year-round availability is a great plus for floral designers who love irises. They can be purchased in the bud or "pencil" stage when a line of color is showing and the green sheath around the bud is beginning to open. *Irises* should not appear wilted or dried out, and the stems should have consistent green foliage with very little yellowing. The foliage is often yellow at the tip, usually due to growing conditions both in greenhouses and outdoors. This discoloration can easily be trimmed away.

The fresh, showy look of irises adds accent and interest to a variety of spring designs. Irises last longest when arranged in vases or containers filled with nutrient solution. Combine *Irises*, Freesias, and tulips in a fresh spring bouquet and place the bouquet in a watering can or cylinder vase. When arranging irises in foam, select floral foam that is specifically formulated for spring flowers and thoroughly soak the foam before positioning it in the container. Irises are lovely in Oriental or line designs and can be arranged in a needlepoint holder. Iris blooms will continue to open within the design, so allow room for the flower to fully develop.

The vase life of an iris is short (three to six days) but spectacular. Never allow the flowers to dry out, whether in a vase or floral foam. Check the stems and rinse away any sand or soil caught between the foliage and stems. Recut the stems and place in a cool floral preservative solution. Iris buds will open if left at room temperature, away from drafts and direct sunlight, and well-hydrated buds will open while in arrangements. Trim any yellowed leaf tips, maintaining a natural-looking shape.

Opposite page: Creating a visually pleasing mix of lines, crisp white irises tower above swirling callas and kangaroo paws in stunning shades of yellow. An elegant silver urn perfectly echoes the bright shades of the flowers, and silver-plated lemons add whimsy to the design.
Design Tip: *When creating a multi-layer arrangement, begin with tall, straight flowers in the center and work outward, varying the angle and length of each "layer" of stems.*

Spectacular peonies command attention in the spring. In floral designs or in the garden, their beautiful form is a treasure for the eye. Peony history dates back to cultivation in China more than 2,500 years ago. Continued breeding has produced hundreds of peony (*Paeonia*) cultivars. Both the common and scientific names are based upon the Greek name for Paeon, the physician to the gods. Paeon was changed into a flower by Pluto in gratitude for Paeon's successful cure of Pluto's battle wounds. The flower's meaning in the language of flowers from the Victorian era is bashfulness or shame.

These large, fragrant flowers can be three to nine inches across and are available as single, semi-double, double, or anemone types. Most peonies are *Paeonia lactiflora*, but a woody stemmed type called *Paeonia suffruticosa* (tree peony) has some limited availability. Early, midseason, and late varieties are available. The foliage is attractively large, lobed, and dark green. Colors include pink, white, rose, peach, red, purple, yellow, and bicolors.

spring peonies

The peony, which gives any arrangement a distinctive emphasis and mass, complements many design styles including traditional, formal, Oriental, garden, and casual. Peonies are lovely all by themselves in a vase arrangement. When designing in floral foam, recut the peony stem before placing it into fully moistened foam and always keep the container completely filled with water.

The flowering season of the peony is short but highly anticipated. Peonies are available from May through July, mainly due to the many varieties' different flowering times. The flowers may be cut or purchased while still in bud. Look for flowers and leaves that are turgid (full of water), not dried out, and uniform in color.

Each flower will last four to seven days. Recut the stems and place them in warm floral preservative solution. Be sure to remove any lower leaves that will be below the water line. When designing with peonies from the garden, brush away any ants, which are merely seeking nectar. For a soft romantic look, peonies may be dried by hanging them upside down. Use their natural dried stems and place them in baskets of other dried flowers to capture spring all year long.

Bouquets of fragrant peonies add newness and vitality to the spring season. From the attractive double types to the graceful single ones, their lovely fleeting beauty enriches the soul.

Opposite page: Several glorious peonies take center stage in this breathtaking, garden-picked gathering that beautifully combines some of spring's most enticing blossoms with rare floral treasures. **Design Tip:** *Distinguish your gardeny floral creations with unusual floral finds from wholesalers as well as local growers and farmers' markets. Combine unique specimens and simple garden varieties with traditional flowers for a wonderfully different presentation.*

Designing with delightful spring flowering branches is a unique pleasure of early springtime. The use of flowering branches in floral design has been employed from very early times. The Chinese and Japanese created designs with them in ancient times. Later, the Europeans positioned colorful branches in their creations. The Victorians gave symbolic meanings to some popular flowering branches—apple blossom means preference and quince conveys temptation.

Branches that can be successfully flowered for use in floral designs are from trees or shrubs that flower before the leaves appear. Many types of fruit trees (apple, cherry, pear, and peach) and ornamental trees or shrubs (crab apple, *Forsythia*, quince, *Spiraea*, and pussy willow) provide excellent flowering branches for spring arranging. Apple (*Malus*) and pear (*Pyrus communis*) are native to Europe and western regions of Asia. Cherry blossoms (*Prunus*) were first enjoyed in Japan. Peach trees (*Prunus persica*) were introduced from China. Native to Japan, Korea, or China, attractive flowering shrubs include pussy willow (*Salix*), flowering almond (*Prunus triloba var. multiplex*), and bridal wreath *Spiraea*. *Forsythia* was hybridized in Germany. Crab apples (*Malus*) are originally from America, Europe, and Asia.

The magnificent blossoms of flowering branches add height and line as well as graceful mass within arrangements. Branches are compatible with many design styles such as garden, Oriental, contemporary, and traditional. Spring branches are beautiful additions to vase arrangements and can also be used alone. Pussy willows, or any flexible branch, can be shaped into a "handle" above a container. Use brown-taped wire or ribbon to keep the handle together and insert each end into opposite sides of floral foam inside the container.

blooming *spring* branches

In late winter and early spring, the swelling buds of flowering trees and shrubs are still months away from blooming but may be harvested and flowered indoors. In later spring, branches can be shipped from northern areas to extend the season. Look for live branches that have numerous buds.

To open flowers, the stems should be recut and placed in containers of warm water away from direct sunlight. Spritzing with mists of water can hasten opening. Flowers may start to appear on the stems within a week or ten days, but it can take up to three weeks for branches like *Forsythia*, which is cut very early in the season. Flowering branches may last five to seven days in a cool, shady, non-drafty spot in the home.

Pussy willows should be cut or purchased before the yellow stamens appear above the catkins (the fuzzy part of flower). When catkins are fully developed, the branches should be kept dry until arranging. Once dried, pussy willows will last for years.

Opposite page: A horizontal pairing of pear branches and cream-colored peonies lends a serene feel to home interiors. Arranged in a French flower pail, this country-style arrangement has a quiet charm all its own. **Design Tip:** *When designing with flowering branches, you don't always have to use them for height; horizontal placements are equally striking.*

At right: Spring blossoms and newly budding boughs combine beautifully, as is demonstrated in this composition of redbud branches, pussy willows, Freesias, carnations, tulips, and sweet Williams. In addition to height, the branches add mass, helping to fill out the design with a minimum of added stems. **Design Tip:** *When designing with branches, use them to create a framework. Once the branches have formed an "outline," fill in the shape with additional blooms.*

Easter is a joyous springtime event, and the holiday captures the essence of the long-awaited season of rebirth and renewal. Easter celebrates the jubilant Christian commemoration of the resurrection of Christ. Another part of this seasonal holiday is the whimsical folklore of bunnies, painted eggs, and of course the flowers of spring. The actual date of Easter is variable from year to year, occurring on the Sunday after the first full moon on or after March 21.

The white trumpet lily, so popular at this holiday, is now called the Easter lily. Palms, spring blooming plants, arrangements of fragrant spring flowers, and mixed gardens of green and blooming plants were all historically popular decorative items for churches and homes. Decorated crosses and flowing masses of Easter lilies form the background for numerous church services at the holiday.

spring
easter

PHOTOGRAPHY BY MARK ROBBINS

Sweet peas, *Freesias, Ranunculuses, Anemones,* lilacs, and callas, along with lovely ivy greenery and trimmed or natural palm fronds, are captivating Easter choices. Spring bulb flowers and plants are especially appropriate and lovely to mark this joyous holiday and the coming of spring. Daffodils, hyacinths, tulips, grape hyacinths *(Muscari),* and lilies make lovely cut flowers and flowering plants. Potted plants including crocuses, delicate netted *Irises,* pansies, azaleas, *Hydrangeas,* heather, *Gloxinias, Cyclamen,* and orchids are wonderful expressions of Easter as are green plants such as palms, ferns, and many others. Flowering branches of dogwood, *Forsythia,* and pussy willow *(Salix)* also add to the feeling of the season.

Today's Easter arrangements and decorations include many beautiful design styles such as formal or traditional, elegant, garden, or playful designs for children. A formal design for church or home might include flowering branches, callas, and white lilies with palms and ferns. Striking contemporary designs using lilies and tulips along with Scotch broom would be another expression of Easter. A garden look for Easter is also popular. Try shaping *Forsythia,* heather, or pussy willow into a circular handle and attaching it to a wicker basket. Add daffodils, grape hyacinths, and *Ranunculuses* as well as Italian *Ruscus,* huckleberry, and moss.

Playful, whimsical designs are instant hits with everyone. Add chicks and eggs into colorful vase arrangements or floral designs to convey Easter cheer. Plush bunnies can be tucked into garden-style designs or planted gardens. Beautifully decorated potted green and blooming plants are always popular gifts and function as decorative items for home or church. Add accessories like branches with birds and nests or chicks, eggs, or bunnies.

Easter embodies the wonderful freshness and newness of spring. From joyous religious celebrations to playful customs such as Easter egg hunting, Easter is a welcomed breath of spring.

*Opposite page: An elegant, gardeny gathering of lilies, tulips, Dianthus, larkspurs, heather, and fresh greens is perfectly displayed in a weathered basket and topped with an unusual crown of pussy willow. **Design Tip:** Adding stems of pussy willow to a simple, low arrangement is a fast way to double the size and, therefore, the impact of the design. Seasonal accessories, such as this charming bunny, can be accessorized to coordinate with your creations.*

*At right: Lush, pink-hued lilies, tulips, hyacinths, and Gerberas are gathered in a variety of contrasting ceramic pots. Varying container heights gives the display a multidimensional feel. **Design Tip:** Springy accessories, like the green-painted eggs, are charming additions to tabletops and other displays. Eggs are also great accents since they can be dyed to add contrast to any design.*

39

A season of newness and hope, spring is the perfect time for brides and grooms to start new lives together. Spring flowers beautifully emphasize love and joy at the wedding ceremony.

The first bouquets of flowers were created for English ladies to take to social events. Eventually, in the Victorian era, brides began carrying bouquets. Each flower and leaf conveyed an emotion and message, based on the language of flowers developed during that time. Some popular spring flowers and foliages and their meanings are apple blossom, preference; purple lilac, first love; white lilac, innocence; lily-of-the-valley, purity or return of happiness; fern, fascination or sincerity; snowdrop, friendship or purity; and sweet pea, delicate pleasures.

The first wedding bouquets were small, round groupings of one type of flower or multi-colored mixtures. Queen Victoria's wedding in 1840 popularized the all-white bouquet. Her wedding flowers were orange blossoms carried in a small bouquet and also added to her veil and gown. Today's bouquets are larger than the earlier flower gatherings. All-white bouquets are still preferred by a majority of today's brides; however, each bride is free to choose colors and combinations to fit her personality and style.

spring weddings

PHOTOGRAPHY BY MAXINE JACOBS

Contemporary or garden-inspired, bouquets create the perfect look for a spring wedding. Bouquets can be simple and elegant, such as classic lilies-of-the-valley gathered and tied with a satin ribbon or a European-style bouquet with tulips and white Guernsey lilies (*Nerine*). White *Irises* create a striking scepter-like bouquet when massed together with the stems bound with elegant ribbons.

Colorful, garden-look bouquets incorporate both spring flowers and foliages with trailing habits and interesting textures. Pink *Ranunculuses*, soft pink peonies, and white snowflakes with ferns and trailing ivy are wonderful examples. Hand-tied bouquets can be placed in vases until the wedding and displayed in attractive vases on the head table at the reception.

Spring flowers with shorter stems can be designed in foam bouquet holders. Combine lovely mixtures of white hyacinths, purple grape hyacinths, pink *Cyclamen*, or sweet peas with tulips and *Freesias*.

Spring flowers create a backdrop of beauty and fragrance for the spring bride. Distinctive altar designs, garden-style guest book designs, and breathtaking reception centerpieces are just a sample of the creative design options for the spring wedding.

At left: A wealth of seasonal selections, including lilacs, tulips, Anemones, and Ranunculuses, are hand tied to form this wonderfully casual yet elegant bouquet that is perfect for nuptial celebrations. **Design Tip:** *With one hand full of flowers, finishing a hand-tied bouquet with raffia or a bow can sometimes be a challenge. Waterproof tape may be easier; it will immediately adhere to the stems and will bind them securely without risk of slipping.*

Opposite page: This simple yet stylish gathering of pink roses uses a traditional round shape that is accented by sprigs of seeded Eucalyptus. Suitable for a variety of dress styles, this timeless bouquet will be a hit with spring brides. **Design Tip:** *For a pretty bouquet holder accent, dip a lace handkerchief in a solution of 50 percent water and 50 percent white glue. Wrap the handkerchief around the bouquet holder's handle and allow it to dry upside down.*

Above: Classic lilies-of-the-valley, simply gathered and tied with luxurious double-faced satin ribbon, sweetly and softly say it all. **Design Tip:** When preparing them for design, leave lily-of-the-valley roots on and simply immerse the plants in water to store them. Dipping the florets in a solution of 50 percent water and 50 percent white glue will prevent wilting but will diminish the flowers' trademark fragrance.

Opposite page: This mass of gorgeous white Freesias will add a wonderful aroma to wedding events. A ring of arrowhead plant leaves adds contrast and conveniently hides the bouquet holder. **Design Tip:** When designing with arrowhead plant leaves, cut the leaves several hours before they will be used and allow them to condition in a bucket of cool water. A coating of aerosol acrylic surface sealer on both sides of the leaves will also prolong the life of the cuttings.

Above: Leafless stems of miniature-bloomed 'Million Stars' baby's breath are densely gathered in layers to form this very vogue, cloud-like bouquet. **Design Tip:** *Some flowers such as baby's breath have been used primarily as filler over the years. Try using a traditional filler flower on its own to make an unusual yet beautiful statement.*

Opposite page: Spectacular white Guernsey lilies (Nerines) surround a lavish mound of white tulips in this chic, hand-tied, European-style bouquet. The smooth tulips and ruffly Guernsey lilies create an eye-catching contrast in textures. **Design Tip:** *When designing with two flowers of the same color, group the flowers for added emphasis. This enhances the texture and shape of each flower.*

Fabric flowers and permanent botanicals, such as blooming branches, are a great way to enjoy spring florals throughout the year. Fabric flowers have come a long way from their crude beginnings in early China centuries ago to today's realistic, botanically correct selections. And practically any type of floral material, especially spring blooms, are available in fabric form. And the types of materials used in their manufacture make them practically carefree, enabling designers to simply shape the stems and place them in containers.

Natural plant materials are also dried or preserved in the springtime at their peak of color, shape, and stage of development. Preserving these materials puts time on hold and allows buyers to enjoy the lovely colors and shapes of spring all year long. Drying plants began in early times to keep and preserve culinary plants for use beyond the regular growing season. Drying plants for the seasoning of food and the dyeing of fabrics were the first priorities before decorative uses became popular.

In the 1850s, the art of pressing flowers became very popular. The pressed flowers were then artistically arranged on paper and framed. Today's pressed flowers might also be used for note cards, bookmarks, and floral designs. Spring everlastings that can be pressed include pansies, forget-me-nots, bleeding hearts, tulips, primroses, dogwoods, spring wildflowers like buttercups, violets, and celandine poppies as well as the thin leaves of most plants including ferns, *Clematis*, hardy geraniums, Japanese maples, and other tree leaves.

For a beautiful three-dimensional effect, lady's mantle (*Alchemilla*), *Leptospermum*, peonies, palms, and bear grass may be successfully dried by hanging the stems upside down. For plant materials that noticeably wilt by hanging, such as daffodils, lilies-of-the-valley, bells-of-Ireland, and *Freesias*, a covering of silica sand works well. Many types of dried and preserved flowers and foliages may be purchased. Rice flower is an example of a spring flower that can be preserved; preserved materials have a soft and flexible quality.

spring
everlastings

Dried, preserved, fabric, and permanent materials may be designed in floral styles ranging from casual, romantic, garden, or formal. For a casual mixture, combine rice flower with *Leptospermum* and bear grass for a wildflower look. To create the casual look of a few flowers floating in a bowl of water, add a preserved or fabric material to acrylic "water." See design on page 49 for a look at this faux wonder.

Spring everlastings and fabric flowers bring memories of the springtime all through the year. Their colors and shapes and botanical realism are delightful in springy floral designs.

Opposite page: This gardeny group of ultra-realistic fabric flowers, in hues both bright and pastel, has as much impact as its fresh counterpart. Massed in a wicker storage box, these silk Hydrangeas, Cosmos, and peonies combine for a cheerful, long-lasting addition to the home. **Design Tip:** *Choose an unusual container that echoes the style of a particular arrangement. Here, the loose, casual style of this garden gathering is complemented by a laid-back wicker box.*

At right: Premade bird's nests, realistically enhanced with feathers and filled with small wooden eggs, are hot-glued atop clay pots that have been artificially aged. **Design Tip:** *For a faux-aged look, spray a terra-cotta pot with soapy water followed by one coat of whitewash paint. While the first coat is still wet, spray the pot again with soapy water followed by a coat of moss green paint. Finally, add another layer of soapy water followed by a coat of basil green paint.*

Opposite page: A striking decorative, this lovely conical flowering dogwood "tree" is as appropriate for Christmas or winter as it is for spring. **Design Tip:** *Place a drop of glue on the center of the back of each dogwood blossom to attach them to the cone. This will leave the petals free and give the tree a ruffly, rather than flat, appearance.*

Below: A graceful and long-lasting centerpiece for casual summer gatherings, dogwood blossoms float lazily in clear glass bowls filled with acrylic "water." **Design Tip:** *Fill a container with acrylic "water" and wait until the material is almost fully set. Then place the blossoms atop the "water" as though they were floating. If the acrylic is too hard, secure the blooms with a spot of glue.*

summer
seasons of flowers

Summer is an ideal time to consider using flowers for outdoor entertaining and interior décor. During this season, Mother Nature provides plenty of inspiration for floral designs—from gorgeous, colorful gardens to sunflowers blooming along the roadways.

Color is perhaps the most important consideration in summer arrangements. Bright, hot hues of red, orange, and yellow are traditional favorites, but cooler colors also make fresh statements. Many summer flowers are available in beautiful shades of blue, pink, or purple.

Summer also brings delicious fragrances to bouquets. Clippings from herb gardens can add spicy, zesty scents while geranium leaves lend an earthier smell.

PHOTOGRAPHY BY MARK ROBBINS

*Above: Perfect for outdoor parties and weddings, this loose, garden-style arrangement is created in a wall basket. Roses, lilies, asters, and Veronica elegantly celebrate the spirit of summer festivities, from casual to formal. **Design Tip:** Lilies are thirsty flowers, so be sure they have a bountiful water source.*

*Opposite page: A trio of cherubs rests beneath a cloud of colorful flowers and foliage. A vibrant collar of Dahlias is the focal point of the arrangement and from it springs a profusion of Trachelium, Salvia, blue lace flower, and maidenhair fern. Glorious tendrils of ivy trail down to the table, where a mass of Hydrangeas completes the ensemble. **Design Tip:** To highlight one flower in a new way, try featuring it en masse, starting at the base of the container and extending its height.*

Opposite page: Texturally diverse, vividly colored flowers are eclectically arranged in this adventurous design. Exotic flowers such as callas, Gerberas, kangaroo paws, waxflowers, and Anemones are perfectly at home with traditional roses in an antique reproduction vase. **Design Tip:** *When arranging bright, hot colors in a dense formation, give the design an airy touch by adding long, leggy flowers such as the kangaroo paws shown here.*

Above: Small, similar designs arranged in multiples can sometimes have a more striking impact than one large design. Filled with sweet peas, tulips, lilacs, Ranunculuses, Viburnums, and Bulbinella, these "baskets" are actually glass vases covered with woven wicker. **Design Tip:** *For small, dense bouquets like these, it is helpful to arrange the blooms in your hand first, then tie them with raffia or waterproof tape, and drop them into vases.*

Opposite page: The simple beauty of monobotanical designs adds an elegant touch to any home. Here, a tall vase of rich blue Delphiniums, combined with lush green broom Ruscus, provide contrast to a low arrangement of yellow Freesias and mint leaves. **Design Tip:** In monobotanical arrangements, the flowers should be arranged first to present a strong statement. Add foliage sparingly to accent, not overshadow, the blossoms.

Below: What better way to welcome guests to your table than with bouquets created just for them. A few tiny Salvia stems make a big impact when set on a plate that echoes their deep, regal color. **Design Tip:** When planning floral arrangements for dinner parties, look beyond the centerpiece design and use flowers to accent the entire table, including plates and napkin rings.

Opposite page: The stately yet casual gathering of lilies, roses, snapdragons, stocks, and Gerbera daisies owes its lighthearted air to the subtle variations of color among the blossoms. Lime green bells-of-Ireland provide eye-catching contrast to the otherwise pale palette of hues from snowy white to golden ecru. **Design Tip:** *In monochromatic designs, use several shades of the same color to give depth to the arrangement.*

Above: A handmade, Americana-style wooden slat basket is a well-chosen container for this lavish, nature-inspired arrangement of 'Pompeii' Oriental lilies, Solidago, Queen Anne's lace, Acacia, and fruited kumquat branches. **Design Tip:** *A mixed mass of flowers needs a strong focal point. Here, the white lilies stand out against the dark greens of the foliage and lend personality to the design.*

59

Above: Nature lovers will adore this casual arrangement of waxflowers and summer cypress in a French flower bucket. The informal, "just-picked" look also makes this design an appropriate companion to country-style home décor. **Design Tip:** When arranging flowers in a metal container, be sure to use a plastic or papier-mâché liner to avoid chemical reactions that could reduce the life of the flowers.

Opposite page: Bring a taste of the garden indoors with a connoisseur's collection of flowers in a suitably outdoorsy container. Chocolate cosmos, globe amaranth, Scabiosa, rice flower, and Freesia fill a weather-rusted bucket with casual grace. **Design Tip:** Cut fresh fern fronds several hours before you will use them in an arrangement. Dip them in a hydrating solution and allow them to "drink" and firm up before placing them in the design.

A planted garden is a lovely way to celebrate summer. The Romans were the first to plant a combination of materials together. During the Dark Ages, monks in monasteries carried on this enjoyment. Examples of today's planted gardens are dish gardens, bulb or specialty gardens, European gardens, and aquatic gardens.

To create a dish garden, plant small green and blooming plants in low containers or lined baskets. For a successful dish garden, select plants with pleasing color and texture combinations and compatible growing needs. Dish gardens can portray a scene or express a theme, such as Oriental, tropical, or desert. Fresh flowers in water tubes, branches, stones, driftwood, or figurines may be added to enhance the theme.

Dish gardens can be enjoyed for months with suitable light exposure and careful watering when the soil is dry beneath the surface. The plants' roots will eventually outgrow the limited soil area of the container and can then be potted individually.

Bulb or specialty gardens are mixtures of plants in containers with drainage holes. Mixed bulbs, selected for varying heights, are planted in the fall and kept cool in winter for flowering in the house during spring. Charming groupings of herbs, ferns, annuals, perennials, or vegetable plants are examples of specialty gardens.

summer planted gardens

PHOTOGRAPHY BY STEPHEN SMITH

European gardens are a lovely variation of the dish garden. To make a European basket, position green and blooming plants, still in their original pots, in pleasing combinations within a lined basket or container to appear as if they are growing that way. Cover the pots' rims with Spanish moss or sheet moss. Combinations of colorful blooming plants, along with upright and trailing foliage plants, add variety and texture to European gardens.

Water planted gardens when the soil beneath the surface feels dry. Avoid overwatering or letting the plants stand in water by using an individual liner for any plant like *Hydrangea* that requires more water than others. Sun-loving plants should be placed in well-lighted areas. Eventually, the individual plants can be separated and then placed throughout the home or garden.

Aquatic or water gardens incorporate floating aquatic plants with cut flowers and foliage. The roots of the aquatic plants are submerged in the water while the plant floats on the surface. Cut plant materials can be added in small floral-foam-filled liners that are secured to the container. These aquatic gardens are tranquil and peaceful—a feast for the eye and the soul.

Opposite page: As the queen of all flowers, roses are perfect gifts. Put a new spin on a classic with a miniature rose bush. The tiny blooms are available in the traditional shades of red, pink, and white. **Design Tip:** *Roses need indirect sunlight to keep their blossoms in perfect condition. Water roses well when the soil is dry to the touch but don't allow them to stand in water.*

At Right: All the treasures of the garden are gathered in this basket. Nestled among the fern and two varieties of azaleas are a decorative salt-stained pot and a robin's nest. **Design Tip:** *Get the look of a planted garden by nestling plants in individual clay pots in a bed of moss. This allows you to water and fertilize each plant according to specific needs.*

*Opposite page: Ideal for containers that are deep and wide, these fantastic fern varieties can be potted together or placed individually in small pots. Because they are easy to care for, ferns make great gifts for those with "not-so-green-thumbs." **Design Tip:** Place a layer of rocks, gravel, or terra-cotta pot shards in the bottom of the container before planting. This keeps the plants from standing in water and provides a reservoir for when the soil begins to dry out.*

*Below: A gathering of colorful Crotons and Dracaenas, artfully arranged and planted in this European colonial-inspired wire basket, is sure to add warmth to any room. And with tender loving care, these plants will thrive for years to come. **Design Tip:** To keep moss in the basket and off the table, line the basket with a sheer hair net before adding moss.*

An elegant aristocrat for summer bouquets, *Delphiniums* add a welcome blue in mixed vase arrangements. The word "delphinium" is from the Greek word meaning "dolphin" because the long spur on the flower is reminiscent of the dolphin's nose. *Delphiniums* were found in Western Europe and East Asia in 1578.

Delphiniums are readily available as two distinct forms—large, showy *Delphinium elatum* and short, loose, butterfly-like 'Belladonna' types. The flower type is a spike-like raceme with small-stemmed florets connected to a central stem. The flower's stem has a beautiful tapered shape that is wider at the base and thinner at the top. The florets open from the bottom up, and each floret has an extended tubular part called a spur.

The largest and showiest *Delphinium* is the classic double-petaled flower, *Delphinium elatum*. Pacific Giants, Blackmore, and Langdon hybrids, as well as the Round Table series, are commonly grown for their striking cut flowers. Their beauty and height are excellent for large, formal, and oversized designs. These linear flowers blossom in rich shades of blue, dark blue, purple, lavender, red, peach, and white. Remove any damaged florets or yellowed foliage before adding to arrangements and avoid pruning the tops of the stems to preserve the elegant tapered shape.

The 'Belladonna' types (*Delphinium x belladonna*) are single-petaled with graceful and distinctive spurs. This hybrid of *Delphinium elatum* was first introduced in 1900. Vivid blue and sky blue describe commonly available colors of this shorter type. These graceful flowers are versatile and well suited to the wildflower look, country-style arrangements, and informal designs as well as traditional creations. Use the spike-like raceme in its entirety in arrangements or trim them into several insertions and add as filler to smaller designs, even wedding bouquets in foam holders.

summer delphiniums

Commercially, *Delphiniums* are readily available nearly year-round. Look for stems with at least one-half of the florets open with good color showing in the buds at the top. Foliage should not be yellow or damaged. The dropping or shattering of florets is a common occurrence; handle the stems carefully and avoid ethylene exposure.

Delphiniums are short- to medium-lived flowers, lasting five to twelve days. Remove the wilted lower florets to maintain a neat appearance. Recut the stems and place them in a fresh vase solution to encourage bud opening and prolong flower life.

A closely related flower is larkspur (*Consolida ambigua*, formerly *Delphinium ajacis*). Larkspurs fill summer bouquets with pink, white, and lavender shades. The fine-textured foliage and slender flowering spikes separate them from *Delphinium*. This lovely flower may be purchased commercially year-round.

Opposite page: The full-blossomed, spiky stems of these stunning Delphiniums form a breathtaking creation in clear glass. Because of the exceptionally large blooms of these varieties, fewer stems are required for a fabulously full effect. **Design Tip:** *Arrange full-flowered stems loosely with the help of a clear glass support mechanism, such as waterproof tape applied in a grid-like fashion or a flat piece of chicken wire clamped across the opening of the vase. Either mechanism will hold the individual stems in place.*

Above: A treasure of flowers in blues and yellows, spiced with touches of lavender and orange, welcomes family and friends from its place of honor amid a blue and white sea of Delft patterns in porcelain and linen. **Design Tip:** *Let the color wheel guide your choices when combining colors in an arrangement. This design features two eye-catching complementary color combinations— blue and orange and purple and yellow.*

Opposite page: This vertical planting of garden favorites is styled with a flair for the natural. Larkspurs, Nerines, waxflowers, and heathers are perfectly arranged to suggest that, instead of being planted, they simply sprung up in this location. **Design Tip:** *Begin with the heaviest materials, like Nerines and larkspurs, in the center and move outward with lighter-weight flowers such as heathers. Use ornamental grasses and foliage as a final touch.*

Above: With a distinctive double sheaf-like styling and a nontraditional color harmony, this noteworthy centerpiece is sure to be a conversation piece as well. Stocks, larkspurs, and Delphiniums beautifully combine with fresh foliages and eye-catching white gourds for an unforgettable presentation. **Design Tip:** *Use six-inch wooden picks to secure gourds to a piece of floral foam. Place them at varying heights and depths for visual interest.*

69

Daisies and the carefree days of summer go hand in hand. The charm of the uncomplicated daisy lies in its center, which provides a beautiful contrast to the petals. In the language of flowers, daisies symbolize innocence. The name "daisy," however, may be used in reference to several different flowers, including the *Gerbera* daisy, daisy mum, and Marguerite daisy.

The *Gerbera* daisy (*Gerbera jamesonii*), also called Transvaal daisy, originated in South Africa and Asia. Borne as a solitary flower on a leafless stem, *Gerbera* daisies are available in single, double, and spider-flowered varieties, and standard and miniature sizes. *Gerberas* come in a festival of fun colors from white to yellow, orange, pink, or red with either light or dark centers (disc flowers). *Gerberas* can be found in both pastels and bright hues, making them perfect for summer designs.

Gerbera daisies can be arranged in floral foam with proper support for the stems—such as wiring and taping—but they will last longer in vase arrangements. Avoid forcing soft *Gerbera* stems into floral foam. Keep the containers well-watered and recut *Gerbera* stems frequently, preferably under water.

Gerberas are available year-round. The centers should have one to two rows of disc flowers showing pollen, indicating flowers in their peak. Look for those with firm healthy stems, particularly in the "neck" area near the flower head, which should not be bent or limp.

summer
daisies

Gerberas may last from five to fourteen days, depending on the cultivar. Use nonfluoridated water, and avoid ethylene exposure. For at least two hours before designing, condition *Gerberas* by resting the flower heads on the lip of a tall container, allowing the stem to hang straight into the solution without touching the bottom.

The daisy chrysanthemum (*Dendranthema x morifolium*) has multiple flowers on each stem in colors ranging from white, yellow, salmon, pink, lavender, and bronze with yellow, green, or brown centers. The anemone or duet type, with its tufted, fuller center, also has the general appearance of a daisy. The Marguerite daisy (*Argyanthemum frutescens*, formerly *Chrysanthemum frutescens*) has several white or yellow daisies per leafy stem.

These smaller daisies may be used as fillers and smaller mass or accent flowers. Daisies are at home in baskets, clay pots, or watering cans. Other garden flowers, such as sunflowers or black-eyed Susans, blend well with daisies. After purchase, recut the stems, removing the lower leaves before placing in designs. Be sure to add cut flower preservative to the water. Daisy mums are very long lasting, usually fourteen days or more. The Marguerite daisy may last five to seven days.

At left: Marguerite daisies, Gerberas, and daisy-like flowers such as spray chrysanthemums and sunflowers make a lavish presentation for a reasonable price. Bits of Solidago add texture and form. **Design Tip:** *Line clay pots with plastic before inserting wet foam and flowers to prevent moisture from seeping through the clay.*

Opposite page: Daisies have a simple beauty all their own, and it is perfectly celebrated with these round-mound-type designs. Arranged in French flower buckets and joined by wispy tendrils of ivy, fresh daisies hint of warm summer breeze, regardless of the time of year. **Design Tip:** *In order to give necessary dimension to round, monobotanical designs, place the flowers at varying heights and vary the directions in which the flowers' faces are turned.*

summer roses

Beautiful, fragrant roses are the most beloved flowers of summer. History records the use of roses as far back as ancient Egypt. In the Roman Empire, thousands of rose petals were strewn lavishly on banquet room floors. Roses are fluent in the language of love, with red meaning "I love you," white meaning "innocence," pink meaning "perfect happiness," and yellow meaning "jealousy" or "decrease of love."

The genus *Rosa* cromprises 100 species and thousands of cultivars in a range of colors including white, cream, pink, yellow, orange, peach, coral, red, lavender, and bicolors. Roses are available as large-flowered hybrid teas, small-flowered sweethearts, and medium-flowered spray roses. Rose stems may be as short as twelve inches or as long as two feet or more. Some roses, particularly lavender-colored varieties, have a lovely fragrance, although many commercial varieties do not.

The rose is a classic cut flower. For a simple and stylish look, float a velvety blossom in a bowl or place a few showy stems in a bud vase. Roses are beautiful in vase arrangements of just one color, called monochromatic designs, or two or more colors blended together. Different types and sizes of roses are lovely placed together within the same arrangement. Rose topiaries in clay or copper pots lend elegance to garden parties or summer weddings.

Before designing with roses, remove thorns and any lower leaves that will be under water or in floral foam. To keep roses from drying out, always leave them in water until they are to be used. Give each stem a fresh cut before placing in designs.

Roses are available throughout the year. Buy only mature roses on which the sepals (the green leaf-like covering over the petals) point outward or downward, not upward, and they shouldn't partially cover the petals. Immature roses may never open. Older roses may look faded or feel too soft. Avoid roses with yellow or damaged leaves. The outermost petals may be bruised or darkened from the stress of shipment; this is normal, and bruised petals should be removed after purchase.

A fresh cut rose generally has a vase life of five to fourteen days. Recut roses under warm water and place them in floral preservative solution. Always keep roses in a water solution, with no leaves under water. You can revive a wilted rose with "bent neck" by submerging the entire stem in warm water and immediately recutting the stem under water. Allow the rose to float for five to ten minutes and the neck will be firm and straight again.

Opposite page: These four exquisite varieties of hybrid tea roses, 'Sahara de Meilland,' 'Terra Cotta,' 'Emma de Meilland,' and 'Exotica' (from left to right), are fairly recent rose-hybridizing developments. All feature impressive bloom sizes, lengthy stems, and, of course, gorgeous color. **Design Tip:** *When displaying a large quantity of flowers, separate the colors for a captivating contrast.*

Above: Create an indoor garden with a petite version of the world's favorite flower. Miniature roses, in terrarium-style plantings, are elegantly showcased in simple bell jars. Pockets of moss in the jars' bases lend to the dish garden effect. **Design Tip:** *When displaying plants in clear glass, use sheet moss to gently wrap the plants' bases, stylishly hiding the roots and soil from view.*

Opposite page: In European-style flower buckets, several different varieties of roses, including 'Delilah,' 'Fancy Amazon,' 'Vogue,' and 'Tickle Pink,' are combined to form a luxuriant monobotanical topiary that features a dynamic color palette. **Design Tip:** *A topiary is a great way to use leftover rose stems. Fill a bucket with floral foam, push a "trunk" of gathered stems into the foam, glue a floral-foam-filled cage onto the trunk's top, and insert flowers.*

Opposite page: This stunning mixed rose arrangement is composed of both sweetheart and spray roses, offering blooms in a variety of sizes. The sweetheart varieties included are 'Pistache,' a soft yellow, and 'Frisco,' a medium yellow. Spray roses included are 'Cream Gracia,' a creamy white; 'Gracia,' a hot pink; 'Lovely Lydia,' a medium pink; 'Lydia,' a soft pink; and 'Surprise,' a peach-colored rose. **Design Tip:** *For a garden-picked look, mix sweethearts, spray roses, and large and small hybrid tea roses.*

Below: Short-stemmed roses in faux-aged, terra-cotta pots are quick and stylish arrangements for hostess gifts or impromptu entertaining. **Design Tip:** *For a faux-aged look, spray a terra-cotta pot with soapy water followed by one coat of whitewash paint. While the first coat is still wet, spray the pot again with soapy water followed by a coat of moss green paint. Finally, add another layer of soapy water followed by a coat of basil green paint.*

Opposite page: The modern topiary design takes on a natural, outdoorsy feel with pale flowers, a sand-textured container, and a wild vine wreath accent. **Design Tip:** *Long-stemmed roses aren't just for vases anymore. Gather the roses together so that the heads form a topiary ball. Bind the stems together just below the heads with raffia or floral tape. Cut the stem ends to the same length and secure them in a floral-foam-filled container.*

Above: A gorgeous color harmony is achieved with these two rose varieties. The sandy hues of 'Safari,' a sweetheart rose, beautifully accent the sumptuous colors of 'Vicki Brown,' a delightful long-stemmed bicolor selection. **Design Tip:** *For a functional, modern look, try arranging cut flowers in common, everyday containers like this chipwood box.*

Opposite page: A romantic, opulent look is achieved by winding a garland of fabric roses around pale candles and clear glass. Perfect for mantle décor or buffet table accent, this trail of flowers will leave a lasting impression. **Design Tip:** *Fabric flowers contain all the mechanics needed to create this elegant garland. Simply weave the wired stems tightly together to form a trailing chain.*

Above: Lovely pale garden roses are combined with a trail of prickly brown Echinacea in this natural, modern design. The flowers are wrapped with rings of curly willow and bittersweet, and the whole creation is accented with river rocks for a look inspired by today's popular water gardens. **Design Tip:** *Arrange fresh materials in floral foam on one side of an arrangement and add river rocks on the other side for a landscape-inspired look.*

Colorful *Zinnias* give warmth and vibrancy to summer floral arrangements. The name *Zinnia* means "thoughts of absent friends" in the language of flowers. Another common symbolic meaning for *Zinnia* is "youth and old age". The Latin name *Zinnia elegans* was named for botanist Johann G. Zinn. A lover of sun and heat, the *Zinnia* is native to Mexico.

Zinnias come in a multitude of colors and sizes. Most have double flowers, but single flowers, resembling daisies, and semi-double types, are also available. The double types may resemble chrysanthemums, *Dahlias*, or cactus flowers with unique, pointed, spike-like petals (ray flowers). Flower sizes range from one to six inches in diameter. Look for countless colors and bicolors, including an attractive green variety called 'Envy.' *Zinnias* with concentric colorations of red and yellow on the petals resemble *Gaillardias* and lend a hot, south-of-the-border look to any design.

Bright-colored *Zinnias* add bold round shape, mass, and focus to designs. Depending on their colors and forms, *Zinnias* are quite versatile, appropriate for informal, garden, or traditional styles. The simple daisy types are great in casual summer bouquets in baskets or pots.

Zinnias like summer heat and sun and are available May through October. Select flowers at their peak with only one or two rows of yellow disc flowers showing in the center. Older flowers will be completely yellow in the center. Flower petals (ray flowers) should be a consistent bright color. Some brown flecking on the leaves due to insects or rust is common, but the leaves should not be extremely diseased or damaged.

summer
zinnias

To arrange *Zinnias*, recut the stems (only a half inch or less is required) and remove the lower leaves so that none are inserted into floral foam or are below the water line in vase arrangements. Remove additional leaves that are brown or damaged. Thinning out a few leaves in a design may add space and give a more pleasing silhouette. An arrangement of *Zinnias* will typically last five to seven days. Changing the vase solution and recutting the stems every two days will help the flowers last longer. Place the flowers in a cool location away from drafts.

Bold, beautiful *Zinnias* command attention among other flowers. Colorful and sunny, they are the perfect choices for summer designs.

Opposite page: Sumptuous, multicolor mounds of Zinnias capture summer's hottest hues, making them delightful accents for summertime decorating. The compact form of these creations makes them versatile enough to be used in a variety of settings and for a multitude of purposes. **Design Tip:** *Wind bird feathers onto beading wire to form an unusual wrapping for floral arrangements.*

At right: A glorious mound of dried Zinnias and Australian daisies is gorgeous for summer and even fall. Here, two bunches of dried baby's breath are placed in the clay pot first to provide support to the delicate Zinnia blooms. **Design Tip:** *Try dried Zinnias for long-lasting arrangements. Because the dried varieties are often sold without stems, you may need to hot-glue Zinnia heads to other sturdy-stemmed, small-headed dried flowers providing the needed stems for arrangement in foam.*

PHOTOGRAPHY BY STEPHEN SMITH

Opposite page: Pale peach roses and ruffly textured Celosias are combined with vibrant Zinnias in a sunny ceramic vase in this vivacious summer design. A wrapping of bright green vines completes the ensemble. **Design Tip:** A collar of pliable vines provides visual continuity between the flowers and the vase and adds life and interesting detail to an otherwise simple design.

Above: Perfect for outdoor summer entertaining, the botanicals in this lush garden-style arrangement appear to have grown naturally in their space, rather than having been placed there. Zinnias, Hydrangeas, Queen Anne's lace, Liatris, and trailing ivies are all part of this richly colored creation. **Design Tip:** Ivies wilt quickly when separated from their roots, so it's beneficial to wrap the roots in plastic bags before placing ivies in arrangements.

Lilies are spectacular in summer bouquets. Their beauty is the show-stopper of many floral designs and summer gardens. The word lily is a shortened version of the Latin name *Lilium*, which comes from the Greek word for the plant, *leirion*. In the Victorian language of flowers, the symbolic meanings of lily are dependent on the color. White lilies stand for purity or virginity. Yellow ones may symbolize either gaiety or falsehood. In Victorian times, orange lilies conveyed hatred. Lilies originated in Asia, Europe, and northern areas throughout the world.

The lovely, graceful lily has six showy pointed petals and sepals, which all appear similar and star-shaped. Lilies are available in numerous bowl-shaped flower forms, such as Asiatic, Oriental, and hybrids. Oriental lilies are large; fragrant; and available in white, pink, or bicolor. Asiatic lilies are smaller in size than Oriental lilies and available in yellows, oranges, reds, and whites. Both Oriental and Asiatic lilies may have dark flecks on the petals. The Easter lily (*Lilium longiflorum*) is white with a trumpet-shaped form. Lily blossoms are borne on short stems and may have upward-, outward- or downward-facing flowers. Many trumpet types face downward.

summer lilies

PHOTOGRAPHY BY MARK ROBBINS

In floral designs, allow plenty of room for buds and partially opened flowers to continue to open. The brown anthers in the center are attractive, but the pollen should be removed as soon as each flower opens to keep it from staining flowers, hands, or clothing.

Lilies are available year-round. A lily should have one or two open flowers at the bottom of the stem with the upper buds closed. Avoid flowers that appear wilted or stems with leaves that are excessively yellow. After purchase, cut a half inch from the stems and place the flowers in a floral preservative solution. Lower foliage should be removed to prevent bacterial growth in the water solution. Avoid ethylene gas exposure.

Each lily flower will last four to six days. An entire stem of lilies may last two weeks, depending on the total number of flowers on the stem. Several flowers may be open on the stem at one time. As each flower fades, remove it and its short stem.

At Left: Pure white lilies make an elegant statement when arranged alone in clear glass. Just a few stems are necessary for a bountiful, up-to-date look. **Design Tip:** *Remove lilies' pollen-bearing anthers to avoid staining clothing and furniture. To remove pollen from fabric, simply brush the stain away with a pipe cleaner or dry brush or lay the fabric in the sun. Don't touch the stain, though; the oil from your skin will make pollen difficult to remove.*

Opposite page: Oriental lilies and tulips are arranged in a traditional style with symmetrical balance, although a contemporary looseness gives this arrangement a comfortable formality. An ornate bronze urn with a wreath motif, the epitome of classicism and tradition, elevates the arrangement with stately sophistication. **Design Tip:** *If pollen has stained any open lily petals, spray the flower heads with an antitranspirant such as Crowning Glory to wash the pollen away. Avoid touching the stains.*

Bright, colorful sunflowers epitomize summer bouquets. Native to the United States, sunflowers symbolize cheerfulness, friendliness, and even adoration according to the Victorian language of flowers. *Helianthus*, the scientific name for sunflower, originates directly from the Greek words "*helios*" (meaning sun) and "*anthos*" (meaning flower).

The large daisy-like flowers are three to ten inches in diameter. The smaller-sized flowers, such as 'Sonia,' may be referred to as mini sunflowers. The petals, called ray florets, may be cream, yellow, lemon yellow, and orange, as well as rich reds, burgundy, and browns. The center of the sunflower (the disc florets) is usually a contrasting black, brown, or green. 'Sunbright' (with a brown center) and 'Sunbeam' (with a green center) are popular golden yellow types. Most sunflowers are single petaled, but doubles, such as 'Teddy Bear,' are available.

Perfect for country-style arrangements, sunflowers add lively accents as well as eye-catching mass to designs. Sunflowers can also "dress up" and lend a bold high-style drama to contemporary designs and vase arrangements. When arranging in vases, remove any leaves that will extend below the water line, and remove any damaged petals or yellowed or damaged leaves. If a sunflower head is bent downward, the flower can be wired, using a heavy 22- or 20-gauge wire to reposition the heavy flower head so it points upward. Cover the wire with floral tape or place wired flowers strategically in designs so the wire is not visible.

The popular sunflower is an annual that grows in summer gardens but is available for purchase year-round. Look for high quality flowers that are fully open with some pollen present in the centers. Sunflowers will not continue to open once they are harvested. The flowers' necks should not be bent down; instead, it should hold the flower upright or facing outward. Some partial yellowing of leaves is common but avoid stems with completely yellowed or brown leaves. Extremely poor leaf quality may indicate that the flower is too old or that it was allowed to dry out after harvesting.

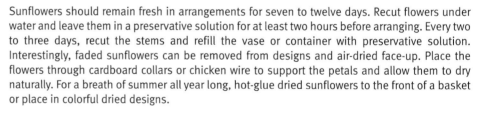

summer sunflowers

Sunflowers should remain fresh in arrangements for seven to twelve days. Recut flowers under water and leave them in a preservative solution for at least two hours before arranging. Every two to three days, recut the stems and refill the vase or container with preservative solution. Interestingly, faded sunflowers can be removed from designs and air-dried face-up. Place the flowers through cardboard collars or chicken wire to support the petals and allow them to dry naturally. For a breath of summer all year long, hot-glue dried sunflowers to the front of a basket or place in colorful dried designs.

Simple and colorful, bold and bright, sunflowers portray both summer fun and sophistication. This beauty is a sure-fire hit for any summer bouquet.

At left: A bright bouquet of wrapped sunflowers is the quintessential summer gift. Perfect for hostesses or "just because" presentations, these radiant flowers are sure to bring a smile to the face of any recipient. **Design Tip:** *Look for unique ways to wrap gift bouquets. Here, we've used stretchy crepe paper and a raffia tie for a stylish presentation.*

Opposite page: A massive collection of sunflowers in a casual, unassuming placement is seasonally accented with the colorful burgundies of Coleus foliage. A simple plastic cylinder vase becomes a "sheaf" when covered with stems of rye grass. **Design Tip:** *Wrap a rubber band around a cylinder vase, then insert stems of rye grass or other dried botanicals. Finally, cover the rubber band with a raffia tie or coordinating ribbon.*

PHOTOGRAPHY BY MARK ROBBINS

Above: Perfectly suited for the easy-going days of summer, these sunflowers add instant cheer to any room. Reminiscent of a van Gogh painting, sunflowers are a natural accent choice for today's popular European country décor. **Design Tip:** *Consider using oversized sunflowers in a small container for dramatic flair. Cut the stems short and cluster the flowers tightly together to form a petite but lush arrangement.*

Opposite page: A topiary of glorious yellow sunflowers is formed by banding the long stems just beneath the flower heads and again at the base. Suitable for buffet tables or outdoor locations, this topiary will make a splash at summer parties. **Design Tip:** *In your hand, arrange the sunflowers to form a topiary ball. Using waterproof tape or waxed string, tie the pliable stems tightly just below the flower heads. Place the topiary trunk in a floral-foam-filled pot and tuck some moss around the stems to hide the foam.*

The elegant calla creates a splendid presence in summer designs. The symbolic meaning for calla is "magnificent beauty" in the language of flowers. The white calla was first seen and recorded in South Africa in 1731. The yellow calla originated in the Transvaal in 1896. Callas are also known as arum lilies, calla lilies, and white arums.

Noble and beautiful, the white calla (*Zantedeschia aethiopica*) reigns as the largest calla, available in traditional white ('Alba') and green or mixed green and white ('Green Goddess'). These callas range from two to four feet in stem length. Several types of miniature callas include yellow (*Z. elliottiana*), pink, red, burgundy, lavender, and purple (*Z. rehmannii*). Mini callas may be 12 to 18 inches in length. The calla flower is an elegant asymmetrical trumpet-shape, called a spathe, with a vivid yellow protruding center containing pollen, called a spadix. Although the calla stem is leafless, the leaves of the calla plant are long, glossy, and heart-shaped.

Callas lend elegance and sophistication to any design. Perfect for summer entertaining, a vase arrangement of callas is a delight to behold. Position a dozen mini callas in a lovely clear vase. For an upscale version of a traditional bud vase, position two or three callas within clear vases on a dining table. Callas are also beautiful in large bouquets or centerpieces for weddings, parties, or special occasions.

Callas' clean lines and sculptural beauty make them the ideal flower to arrange and display in clear glass. The stems are pliable, lending themselves to a variety of design applications. Callas may also be designed in floral foam. To avoid damage, do not force the soft stem into the foam. Use another firmer and slightly smaller stem to make an initial opening in the foam before inserting the calla stem.

summer callas

In days past, callas were exclusively a spring flower, grown in cool greenhouses. However, growers in New Zealand, California, and Ecuador have now made it possible to obtain callas almost year-round. When purchasing callas, select flowers at the stage of opening desired, from tubes to fully open flowers. Calla flowers do not continue to develop or open after harvesting. Some pollen should be present on the spadix, but the spadix should not be completely covered with pollen, which would indicate an older flower. The flower surface should not appear overly wrinkled or discolored.

Calla vase life ranges from five to fifteen days. A calla stem should be recut every two to three days to keep the ends from splitting and rolling up. Replenish and freshen the floral preservative solution to inhibit bacterial growth.

Opposite page: Simple yet dramatic, this lush gathering of brightly colored callas (Zantedeschia) will be a treasured gift. The brilliant pinks and yellows of the callas' petals, called spathes, contrast perfectly with an aged silver pot. **Design Tip:** *Flowers arranged close together are prone to rapid decomposing. Properly mixed nutrient solution will help prevent the flowers' early demise.*

At right: Callas, in a mouth-watering yellow hue, are swirled around inside a clear glass vase to showcase both the spathes and the long elegant stems, which are part of calla's appeal. **Design Tip:** *To give calla stems a graceful arch, stroke the stem in a curving motion. As the stem warms, it becomes more pliable and will bend to fit a variety of containers.*

PHOTOGRAPHY BY STEPHEN SMITH

Below: Capturing the calla's striking sculptural form and demonstrating its beauty when used in clean, simple designs, this bubble-bowl-style creation can enhance a contemporary home or decorate for an intimate gathering. **Design Tip:** *Look for simple but elegant ways to arrange flowers. With callas, use the exceptionally clean, smooth stems as an integral part of the floral composition, and you will find new ways to display these exotic beauties.*

Opposite page: With a surprising yet stunning combination of colors, the bright greens of bells-of-Ireland contrast exquisitely with the deep, dark hues of miniature callas and chocolate cosmos in this elegant arching composition. **Design Tip:** *In a flat, fan-shaped arrangement, add the thin, spiky flowers to the vase first to give shape and framework to your creation. Then fill in the design with more delicate floral selections.*

Opposite page: A multicolor grouping of miniature callas, arranged in a low bowl, is a divine dressing for a coffee table. The callas' supple stems, which simply wind around the inside of the bowl, are pliable, lending themselves to a variety of design applications. **Design Tip:** *If calla blossoms are still tightly closed after purchase, gently push a cotton ball inside the spathe and allow it to remain there overnight. The cotton should force the flower to open.*

Below: The stately blooms of the popular creamy-white calla, commonly known as the white arum lily, are arranged in a bunch with the stunning 'Green Goddess' variety for a dynamic vase presentation. These standard-size callas feature stems that range in length from 24 to 48 inches. **Design Tip:** *For maximum bloom visibility, graduate the grouping by placing the shorter-stemmed blossoms in the front and the longer-stemmed selections in the back.*

In the early 1900s, Mother's Day was started by Anna Jarvis, of Philadelphia, to honor her mother. Miss Jarvis chose the second Sunday of May because that was the day that she lost her mother in 1906. Anna Jarvis started a grass roots effort to make Mother's Day a national holiday. With the help of the floral industry, Mother's Day officially became a national holiday in 1913.

Originally, Miss Jarvis chose the white carnation to be worn by everyone to honor mothers. By 1919, *Florists' Review* promoted the wearing of "white flowers for mothers gone and bright flowers for mothers living." Turn-of-the-century floriculturists recognized that promoting only white carnations to honor mothers was a distribution and marketing nightmare in the making.

Giving mothers their favorite flowers soon replaced wearing carnations to honor her. Popular early gifts included boxed flowers and blooming lily-of-the-valley or geranium plants. Corsages were very popular gifts. Early corsages included carnations, gardenias, sweet peas, or violets, followed in later years by roses and orchids. Soon, mothers were receiving cut flower arrangements in pottery or baskets.

summer mother's day

Flowers for a Mother's Day design can be as varied as the mothers themselves. Classic designs may feature roses, lilies, or daisies. Other eye-catching flowers, such as *Alliums*, *Alstroemerias*, *Anemones*, callas, *Hydrangeas*, *Ranunculuses*, and Queen Anne's lace are sure to please for Mother's Day. Intimate arrangements could include small or fine textured flowers such as heather, spray roses, sweet peas, *Limonium*, miniature carnations, grape hyacinths, *Ixia*, baby's breath, and *Acacia*. Garden flowers are a great floral expression for Mother's Day. Select tulips, lisianthuses, snowball *Viburnum*, or sunflowers for a fresh garden look.

Today's floral gifts for mothers include arrangements of all styles. A romantic, sentimental mixture of pink and white flowers and fillers in a small ceramic vase or a sophisticated design of callas in a flared cylinder vase are both suitable expressions of appreciation. A floral creation emphasizing gardening or nature could combine garden flowers with clay or decorated pots, gardening tools, seed packets, birds, and birdhouses. Decorated plants or planted gardens are also great options for gardening moms. Collectible containers and vases are popular as keepsake gifts. Reminiscent of earlier Mother's Days, antique reproduction containers, such as wire baskets, Victorian handled baskets, or porcelain containers, are also fashionable. Baskets in a variety of shapes, materials, and styles continue to be popular for Mother's Day flowers.

The idea of setting aside a day to show appreciation and love for mothers began with one woman in the early 1900s. From those humble beginnings, Mother's Day has become a very important holiday for expressing love and affection with flowers.

PHOTOGRAPHY BY STEPHEN SMITH

At left: A twig-style teapot can be a quick gift for Mother's Day when filled with a drop-in bouquet of assorted, colorful Gerberas. **Desigh Tip:** *Especially for Mother's Day, teapots, mixing bowls, and other kitchen accessories make wonderful containers that offer keepsake gifts sure to be appreciated by recipients.*

Opposite page: This elegant Mother's Day arrangement is a compact version of the generally loose garden style. A symphony of color is played out with pale peach roses, pure purple hyacinths, red chrysanthemums, yellow Solidaster, and brilliant green foliage. **Design Tip:** *When arranging delicate-stemmed hyacinths in floral foam, use a knife to make stem-sized holes in the foam before insertion. This will prevent stem stress and breakage.*

Above: A casual gathering of pansies, grape hyacinths (Muscari), and Sweet Williams is a wonderful gift for Mom. The bright colors are an eloquent expression of love, and the small size of the vase makes it easy for Mom to display this pretty creation anywhere. **Design Tip:** When arranging with delicate pansies, spray the blossoms with an antitranspirant, such as Crowning Glory, to maximize vase life.

Opposite page: Glorious hues of yellow, pink, purple, and green are artfully combined in this gardeny basket arrangement of pansies, roses, larkspurs, and Scabiosa. Well suited to a variety of home décor styles, this beautiful design would make a wonderful gift for any mother. **Design Tip:** Add life and dimension to a basket design by allowing ivy to trail from the container as it would naturally. Wrapping a few ivy tendrils around the handle completes the look.

PHOTOGRAPHY BY STEPHEN SMITH

Above: The soft pastels of spray and standard roses are gloriously enhanced by the subtle shades of Viburnum blossoms, Alliums, and vining jasmine. Elegantly woven around the handle of this antique celebration basket are vines of flowering quince and coral pea. **Design Tip:** To find the perfect containers for Mother's Day designs, take a look into the past. Browse antique stores for nostalgic baskets and vases full of old-fashioned charm.

Opposite page: Arranged in Biedermeier style, rows of carnations, sweet violets, roses, and spikes of heather have old-fashioned appeal in an antique reproduction wire basket. Vining jasmine is a pleasing complement to this timeless classic. **Design Tip:** Add flair to a traditional Biedermeier arrangement by using a linear flower like heather at the top for a modern, fountain-inspired look.

Weddings with beautiful brides and lovely flowers are summertime events to cherish. Summer offers flexibility as well as beauty and abundance of plant materials. A summer wedding can be a garden party outdoors or a contemporary or traditional ceremony indoors.

Flowers have adorned the bridal couple and ceremony for centuries. The wedding bouquet is traced back to the English, particularly during the Victorian era. Popular summer flowers and foliages and their symbolic meanings in the language of romance are as follows: *Anemone*, anticipation; orange blossom, fertility and happiness; red rose, I love you; white rose, you're heavenly; red and white roses together, unity; and sage, domestic virtue.

summer weddings

The classic round bouquet is reminiscent of the early gathered wedding bouquets of the Victorian era. Today's bouquets can be designed in foam bouquet holders, which keep flowers fresh longer. Bouquet shapes can be round, oval, or cascade. Glorious mixes of *Zinnias*, marigolds, Queen Anne's lace, fully open roses, safflower, and stocks capture the feeling of a summer garden. Other gardeny combinations are *Dahlias*, *Alliums*, and bee balm (*Monarda*) with the filigree texture of scented geraniums.

For a contemporary look for the round bouquet, combine fully open flowers with no foliage. Roses, lilies, or callas would be good choices for contemporary designs. Densely layered 'Million Stars' baby's breath creates a very vogue, cloud-like bouquet. For a traditional look, florists may combine roses and daisies or lilies, *Stephanotis*, and baby's breath.

To design large bouquets, two slanted-handle bouquet holders can be taped together with waterproof tape. After all of the plant materials are inserted, the handles are camouflaged by a wrapping of satin ribbon.

Let summer colors and fragrances come alive for summer wedding ceremonies. Simple or elegant, gardeny or traditional, summer flowers make a wedding memorable for all who attend.

Opposite page: Glorious colors reminiscent of a late summer garden are captured in this magnificent bridal bouquet. Its loose, oval, garden-gathered casualness and mouth-watering color harmony are achieved with 'Royal Ambience' roses, Zinnias, marigolds, stocks, safflowers, Queen Anne's lace, and miniature spray chrysanthemums. **Design Tip:** *When combining bright flowers in a bouquet like this one, add a few white selections to punctuate the other colors.*

At right: Hand-tying is perhaps the preferred method for arranging delicate-stemmed flowers such as the Iceland poppies and windflowers (Anemones) in this gorgeous nosegay. In rich reds, hot pinks, brilliant yellows, and pure whites, this bouquet shines as brightly as the sun on a summer wedding day. **Design Tip:** *Begin constructing this bouquet with a mound of baby's breath to create a support structure for the lightweight Iceland poppies and windflowers.*

PHOTOGRAPHY BY STEPHEN SMITH

105

Opposite page: A traditional round wedding bouquet takes on a sexy, exotic look with creamy white and pink Cymbidium orchids. Suitable for brides and maids alike, this eye-catching design will complement dresses of almost any style. **Design Tip:** *Use floral paint to create a perfect match between flowers and attire. To better match this coral pink dress, the lavender pink orchids were sprayed with light touches of yellow floral paint.*

Below: Proving that great things do come in small packages, this petite bouquet of lavender roses, pink Zinnias, and fragrant white Freesias is just the right choice for modern brides who desire an understated yet elegant floral accent. **Design Tip:** *For an airy, summery look, try adding a lightweight tulle bow to bridal bouquets instead of a heavier ribbon.*

PHOTOGRAPHY BY NATHAN HAM

107

PHOTOGRAPHY BY STEPHEN SMITH

Above: Monochromatic bouquets are made more dramatic when incorporating a wide range of hues from within the color family. Here, purples, from almost-white lavender to violet, are found in Freesias, statice, roses, asters, and lisianthuses. A regal purple ribbon trimmed in gold completes the elegant bouquet. **Design Tip:** Try using an assortment of colors from the same color family and even reaching into adjacent families—like blue and pink—to create an exciting color theme.

Opposite page: Two beautifully scented wedding favorites, white lilacs (Syringa) and lavender roses, are gathered and hand-tied in sections to create a stunning two-tier, garden bouquet. Although the bottoms of the stems are left exposed, as with many hand-tied bouquets, the upper section of the stems is wrapped with luxurious ribbon to provide a convenient place to grasp the bouquet. **Design Tip:** In hand-tied bouquets, the flowers don't always have to be mixed; try segregating them for a contemporary look.

Practically every summertime flower or material imaginable, including succulent summer fruits and vegetables, is available as a fabricated permanent botanical. For summertime arrangements, buy only seasonal selections and combine them in arrangements as if they were fresh. Be sure to buy line, form, and filler flowers as well as feature flowers. Reshape fabric flower blossoms after unpacking by holding them over a steamer for a few seconds to soften the fabric. A steamer may also be used to open a semi-open flower more fully. Be sure to bend and shape wired stems and foliage for a realistic appearance.

The practice of drying plants began with the very earliest cultures. These early people realized the value of plants for medicinal and culinary use and preserved them for use beyond the regular growing season. Summer would have been an important time to harvest and dry many of these plants. Later, plants were also dried for decorative uses.

Summertime is an outstanding time to dry or preserve a wealth of materials. Gardens and roadsides overflow with countless types of flowers and grasses. From the garden, select *Celosias*, larkspur, blue *Salvia*, globe amaranth, yarrow (*Achillea*), statice, sea lavender (*Limonium*), strawflowers, baby's breath, roses, *Zinnias*, marigolds, the seed heads of love-in-a-mist (*Nigella*), poppies, and Siberian *Irises*. Herbs may also be collected for drying. Cattails, wheat, grasses, and horsetail (*Equisetum*) are in an excellent stage to dry during the summer months.

When drying materials, pick those at their peak for color or flowering. Some plant materials easily dry when hung in small bunches upside down in a dry, well-ventilated area away from direct sunlight. Daisy flowers such as sunflowers and black-eyed Susans dry well when placed face-up through a wire mesh with the stems dangling. Drying by the covering method is great for flowers that wrinkle or lose volume, such as roses or black-eyed Susans. Many roses are commercially freeze dried, resulting in a very natural-looking flower. A glycerin solution works well to preserve foliages such as holly, *Magnolia*, or fall leaves, giving the plant material a flexible, non-brittle texture.

summer everlastings

Keep dried everlastings and permanent materials away from direct sunlight. Typically, dried materials may last one or two years and preserved foliages may last one to ten years. With proper care and appropriate in-home placement, fabric flowers and botanicals can last for years.

To dust and care for everlastings arrangements, use a hair dryer on a low, cool setting or spray lightly with an aerosol cleaner formulated for dried flowers. To clean fabric flowers, simply wipe them clean or spray them with a commercial cleaner designed especially for fabric flowers.

Opposite page: Sure to please even the most discriminating recipient, this garden-inspired gathering of fabric roses, in an airy, elevated wire basket, will provide years of enjoyment in the home. **Design Tip:** *Fabric roses will look more realistic if you bend the stems slightly and shape the leaves, arranging them to look like real rose bush cuttings.*

At right: Framing an exquisite collection of preserved roses, these novel frames, formed of dried Equisetum, are premade and sold with stands for easy in-home placement. The completed designs are suitable for year-round display in today's contemporary living spaces. **Design Tip:** *Glue a piece of cardboard onto the back of the Equisetum frame and glue in freeze-dried roses.*

Above: With an aged look inspired by old tapestries and paintings, today's new decorator colors are particularly effective in "period" or antique settings. This subtle tufted mound arrangement is perfect for placing amid a collection of heirlooms. **Design Tip:** *When decorating with a variety of silk flowers, a compact, tightly packed arrangement results in a lush, full look.*

Opposite page: A lavish topiary of lilacs, Hydrangeas, Zinnias, and lotus pods, in green hues from light and bright to dark and shadowed, imparts a fresh, summery feel to any environment. With an almost rectangular form and an unusual multistem trunk, this composition is doubly stunning when used in pairs. **Design Tip:** *Twisted curly willow forms the trunk of this topiary and supports a piece of floral foam in which permanent botanicals are arranged. Discarded flower stems give interesting texture when included in the design.*

Below: Although the raffia-enhanced slat basket and colorful broom blooms add a hint of country, the hanging Amaranthus and custom-painted seed balls, some atop hourglass vases, play an unmistakably retro refrain. **Design Tip:** *For an interesting multitextured look, place tufts of dyed broom bloom in a basket, keeping the color blocks separate and then carefully nestle the seed balls into the colorful bed.*

Opposite page: A sleek, modern bowl, shaped like an inverted triangle, is a suitably elegant resting place for this compact arrangement of dried and permanent botanicals. In a glorious hot pink hue, the design's feature flowers are actually hand made from wood chips and stained for deep, rich color. A fluffy bed of dried star flowers and jazildas lends support to the faux blossoms. **Design Tip:** *Use a fluffy collar of moss to finish the arrangement with flair.*

PHOTOGRAPHY BY STEPHEN SMITH

114

Opposite page: With its modern styling, this "column" of permanent fruits, vegetables, and florals, arranged in a rusty flower bucket, will quickly update classic American country interiors. **Design Tip:** *Place a gathering of faux fruits and vegetables front and center to create a focal point and add hot country-inspired flair to designs.*

Above: For nature lovers, you can't beat this warm, rustic gathering of poppy pods tied with a banding of braided raffia. **Design Tip:** *Particularly when working with dried and permanent flowers, vases are not always necessary for eye-catching designs. When a water source is not needed, try using the flowers' stems to support the structure.*

autumn
seasons of flowers

As the weather turns cooler, autumn brings a glorious, earthy color palette of rusted reds, harvest golds, and pumpkin oranges. Potted mums appear on every neighbor's doorstep, and dried and preserved materials capture the season's unparalleled beauty for months to come.

Some of fall's most wonderful offerings include chrysanthemums of all colors and shapes and the immensely popular Hydrangeas. Many summer favorites also make an appearance during autumn. These include marigolds, lilies, roses, and sunflowers. Texture is another of autumn's wonderful gifts, with materials such as rich red Hypericum berries, golden grains, pumpkins, gourds, and vines.

Dried and preserved materials can be used on their own or incorporated into fresh designs. Look for dried leaves, hybrid corn, cattails, pods of all varieties, and acorns.

*Above: Permanent and dried lotus pods, along with several stems of dried cobra lily, form the focal point of this wall décor piece. Stems of dried wheat and preserved ferns radiate from the center. **Design Tip:** Cut a foam sphere in half and secure the flat side to a wall by attaching a wire hanger. Arrange dried and preserved materials so that they radiate from the center.*

*Opposite page: Eye-catching color and texture abound in this gardeny creation. Mums, carnations, Hydrangeas, Freesias, kangaroo paws, and berried branches combine for a symphony of color including shades of red, yellow, and green. **Design Tip:** Use a spindly branched material like kangaroo paw to add height and dimension to tightly arranged groups of flowers for a more impacting display.*

Opposite page: In a small handled trug, rye grass is interspersed with montbretia foliage to form a fan-shaped sheaf that, for support, may be tied with raffia to the trug's handle. Montbretia blooms, as well as saxicola, coleus, and apples, provide a much-needed color addition to the two-sided design. **Design Tip:** *Physical balance can be challenging when weighty materials such as fresh fruit are incorporated into designs. Making such arrangements two-sided will keep them upright and will allow them to be viewed from all sides.*

Above: Fall-colored flowers speak for themselves when arranged simply in clear glass vases. Here, roses, Nasturtiums, wheat, bittersweet, and Sandersonia, in hues of red, orange, yellow, and pale gold, create an unexpected grouping perfectly suited to casual décor or early autumn outdoor entertaining. **Design Tip:** *Groupings of flowers in clear glass vases are common sights in flower shops. Apply the same concept to bring this treat for the eyes to home decoration.*

Below: Lovely blue and white delft vases hold a mixture of brightly colored fall garden flowers, including multi-colored Ranunculus, sprigs of Veronica and Salvia, and yarrow. **Design Tip:** *This sort of arrangement is perfect for decorative vase collectors. Holidays and parties are a perfect time to pull them from the shelves and show them off.*

Opposite page: Roses, Gerberas, kangaroo paws, and lilies are massed together in a low urn for a celebration of fall color. Deep blue Anemones, which create complementary color harmony with the other blossoms' orange shades, establish a visual link to the container. **Design Tip:** *Add a bowl of gourds and miniature pumpkins as an accent piece brimming with fall charm.*

Opposite page: Stately and elegant, this garden-style arrangement in rich fall hues is perfectly suited to evening entertaining. In rusted reds, sandy peaches, and antique pinks, Gerberas, roses, Gloriosas, and lilies explode from an antique urn. **Design Tip:** *When assembling a large display of color, don't forget to extend the design to the tabletop. Accessorize with figs, petals, and pine cones for a European still-life look.*

Above: As the fall days and nights begin to turn colder, this sunny gathering of lilies, Dahlias, callas, and roses is sure to add warmth to any home environment. **Design Tip:** *Allow lily buds to extend the form of this loose, natural bouquet. As the buds open, the bouquet will be transformed, changing shape in a botanical metamorphosis.*

127

Above: Pink roses and lilies, creamy carnations, dried grains, and various fresh vegetables beautifully combine for an unexpected fall color scheme. More vegetables accent the sand-colored vase, which is reminiscent of the color of harvest wheat. **Design Tip:** Don't count pastels out for fall. Parsnips, cabbages, and squash in shades of beige, purple, and pink give fall a fresh look.

Opposite page: An eclectic testament to autumn's bounty, this fabulous wreath contains a profusion of fruits and vegetables. Dried lemons and limes, freeze-dried gourds, Hydrangeas, globe amaranths (Gomphrena), Proteas, and dried heather are set off by a wide satin ribbon and fall-colored feathers. **Design Tip:** Bind clusters of heather onto a wreath form with a wire wrapping. Make sure the heather is placed so that it flows in a circular formation. Add round forms and then line materials, accenting the spiral form of the wreath.

Opposite page: A wealth of eye-catching texture is presented in a monochromatic, low bowl arrangement. Ringed with a garland of California jasmine, clusters of Celosia, poppy pods, pon pon, Dendranthema 'Kermit,' artichokes, China berries, and Scabiosa pods are presented in the hues of green and brown that only nature can provide. **Design Tip:** *Arrange various materials of the same variety in segregated clusters in order to show off individual textures.*

Above: Starting with a thick sheaf of assorted natural-colored dried grains and grasses, a woodsy design is created with the addition of preserved hanging Amaranthus, miniature ears of corn, and ring-necked pheasant feathers. The color harmony and textural diversity are further enhanced with loops of mesh and striped ribbon. **Design Tip:** *Begin with a thick sheaf of dried materials. Hot-glue other materials into the base to add customized charm.*

Spending a sunny afternoon in a pumpkin patch is a quintessential autumn activity. Picking the best jack-o'-lantern always reminds us of the season of harvest and plenty. Hand-in-hand with thoughts of pumpkins are colorful and unusual gourds. The bounty of autumn brings to mind both of these members of the genus *Cucurbita*. Pumpkins originated in southern Mexico and Central America; gourds are native to northern Mexico and the eastern United States.

autumn pumpkins

The pumpkins most prized for fall decorating are the small and medium sized jack-o'-lantern types. Some smaller varieties include 'Small Sugar,' 'Spookie,' the white-fleshed 'Little Boo,' and the perfectly round 'Mini Jack.' Pumpkin colors range from the popular orange to white to green-striped orange types. Gourds—such as the nest egg, bottle, orange, pear, warted types and the very popular miniature pumpkin-like ones—delight the eye with their unusual variety of forms and colors. Gourds are hard-shelled, ornamental fruits found in many colors such as green, white, orange, and red. They are also available in color patterns including striped, mottled, and banded.

Pumpkins can be used two ways in decorating and creating floral designs. First, pumpkins can be placed within designs or at the bases of designs as accessories. Second, pumpkins can be carved and used as containers for floral designs. If coated with melted paraffin, pumpkins used as containers will last longer. When using pumpkins as containers, line them with foil, plastic, or another lightweight container that fits into the pumpkin's opening. Moistened floral foam can then be placed inside. The "lids" can also be added at the bases of designs as accessories or placed within designs by inserting wooden picks through the flesh before positioning in floral foam.

Because of the hard outer shell, gourds cannot be carved but can be added in their entirety to wreaths or floral designs or placed near containers as accessories with other fall decorations. Secure gourds in designs by applying hot glue to their surfaces and nestling them into wreaths. Gourds can also be mounted by making a hole with a nail and hot-gluing a wooden pick in its place.

Pumpkins and gourds add lively colors, shapes, and textures to autumnal floral displays. Thoughts of autumn are entwined with the selection and displaying of colorful pumpkins and eye-catching gourds.

Opposite page: A hollowed-out pumpkin is an ideal container for a bounteous gathering of autumnal elements. This creation, arranged in wet foam, features montbretia pods, croton leaves, and various green foliages. **Design Tip:** *If coated with melted paraffin, the pumpkin's interior will not deteriorate as quickly, enabling a longer-lasting fall display.*

Above: Flowers showcase fall colors beautifully, but a pumpkin makes a seasonal statement all its own. Roses, Hydrangeas, and bittersweet surround the ultimate icon of fall in this festive basket design. **Design Tip:** *Use a pumpkin as a design element for fall creations. Place it in the basket first, then arrange flowers all around to make the pumpkin look as though it is nestled in gorgeous blossoms.*

Opposite page: The bounty of harvest is elegantly represented in this seasonal wreath. Ears of corn, gourds, miniature pumpkins, and other autumnal accents are hot-glued to a premade wreath form for a stylish fall door piece. **Design Tip:** Often discarded or ignored, dried corn leaves have interesting color and texture. Use them as design elements for extra body and movement.

Above: The epitome of autumn, this lavish buffet piece, handsomely complemented by pumpkins, gourds, and an assortment of fall leaves, demonstrates the glory and bounty of the season. **Design Tip:** For autumn flair on a smaller scale, nestle a pumpkin into a bed of fall leaves placed atop a stately urn.

Wheat sheaves are beloved symbols of harvest bounty. A wheat sheaf is a gathered and tied cluster of dried wheat stems that fan out in a rounded fashion. As decorations, wheat sheaves have been popular for centuries. Wheat, or *Triticum*, probably originated in the Euphrates Valley about 7000 B.C. and is one of the world's oldest and most important cereal crops. In the language of flowers, wheat conveys friendliness or riches.

Wheat grows on a long hollow stem with a head that looks like a beautiful braid. Long slender awns, or bristles, project from the head. The natural color of dried wheat is tan; however, wheat is commonly bleached white or dyed other colors such as orange or golden. One striking variety has black awns and is referred to as black beard wheat. Other cereal grains, including rye and oats, may also be gathered into sheaves.

Wheat sheaves may be created as freestanding designs or incorporated into designs. To give the appearance of a sheaf, a container can be entirely covered with wheat stems that have been rubber banded and tied with raffia. Create a freestanding wheat sheaf by gathering and tightly holding three bunches of wheat while pulling the outer stems downward so that the heads flare outward. Secure the sheaf with a twist tie, adding decorations at the binding point. Large wheat sheaves used in moistened floral foam will need support (like a plastic extender or wooden stake) to prevent the stems from taking up water and bending or collapsing.

Small wheat sheaves may be attached to a wood pick and tucked into fall arrangements. Single stems may be added to autumn centerpieces. A thick sheaf of wheat and other assorted dried grains and grasses make a glorious seasonal door piece. Seasonal additions of pheasant feathers, miniature ears of corn, and preserved *Amaranthus* add textural interest.

PHOTOGRAPHY BY STEPHEN SMITH

autumn sheaves

Dried wheat is available year-round and is very long lasting. Look for wheat that has the desired stem length and seed head color. Dried wheat stems or sheaves should be stored or displayed in a dry, airy environment away from direct sunlight.

The popular wheat sheaf is a glorious reminder of autumn. Its form and line are distinctive and welcoming for decorating and entertaining in autumn.

Opposite page: Simplicity still makes an impressive statement as is demonstrated by this handsomely decorated sheaf of wheat. Only a trio of lightweight freeze-dried miniature pumpkins and an autumn-hued silk bow are needed to finish the design with style. **Design Tip:** *To create the sheaf, three bundles of wheat are gathered and held tightly while the stems are pulled downward until all heads are at the same level and flare outward. A twist tie secures the sheaf.*

Above: A tall, topiary-like sheaf of rye is accented by a ring of lilies, montbretia, and coleus. Green figs, coleus, and lily blossoms adorn the base of this eye-catching design, which, due to a short vase life, would be best suited for parties and special events. **Design Tip:** *This tall sheaf is actually a gathering of dried rye stalks surrounding a floral extender. A foam cage, in which the fresh botanicals are arranged, is placed atop the extender.*

Above: Bearded wheat receives a new and interesting treatment in this elegantly understated pot while a simple tie of ribbon gives the natural design a gender-neutral appeal. **Design Tip:** Cut the wheat short and nestle it into a pot. To secure the stems, dip them into pan-melt glue prior to placement. Trim the tops for a simple and ordered look.

Opposite page: A spray of bearded wheat, arranged in a fanned fashion, tops a column of fresh roses, Freesias, asters, Saxicola, coleus, and red huckleberry, all of which is accented by plums and bosc pears. Although columnar in form, this abundant arrangement, rich in color and texture, seems inspired by the manner of Flemish still-life artists. **Design Tip:** A simple jute bow perfectly accents this design by picking up the pale gold color of its wheat topper.

Colorful chrysanthemums are the quintessential flowers of autumn. Their welcoming warm colors and interesting shapes add to the festive fall scene. Chrysanthemum means golden flower in Greek. In the language of flowers, chrysanthemum (*Dendranthema*) conveys cheerfulness. White mums symbolize truth; yellow mums mean "slighted love." Dating back 2000 years to China, the mum appeared in many early paintings and carvings. To this day, the Japanese imperial family decorates the throne and coat of arms with chrysanthemums.

autumn
mums

Innumerable tints and shades of every color except blue make chrysanthemums the second most popular flower worldwide. Although warm colors predominate, mums are also available in white, lavender, green, and eye-catching bicolors. The brown or green centered mums are currently the fashionable choices. Flower types include spray varieties with multiple smaller flowers such as daisy, cushion, button, and anemone or duet types as well as standard varieties with a single large flower such as the "football" or "spider."

Chrysanthemums lend their autumnal flair to traditional, Oriental, garden, and casual designs. Mums add mass to most designs, with the larger types lending a bolder emphasis and the smaller ones providing accents and filler. Flowers in sprays can be used individually in smaller designs or positioned as entire stems in larger designs.

Chrysanthemums are available year-round in many varieties and colors. Purchase mums that have uniform color and healthy-looking petals and leaves. Mum foliage should be a uniform dark green and not yellowed. After purchase, recut the stems with sharp, clean scissors or a knife; never tear or break off the stem ends. Remove any damaged petals or flowers from the stems as well as any leaves that will be under water.

The most outstanding attribute of chrysanthemums is their long vase life. With proper care, the flowers will last for two to three weeks and still look remarkably fresh. Periodically recut the stems and change the nutrient solution.

The classic chrysanthemum is an integral part of the festive autumn season. With its awe-inspiring palette of colors, types, and textures, the mum fits into numerous fall designs and decorating styles.

*Opposite page: Mixed varieties of mums are clustered in tufts of fall colors. Bronze, burgundy-red, and golden blossoms are accented with orangy-red Pyracantha berries, ivy, and Oregonia leaves. **Design Tip:** A few loops of flax make a dynamic statement. Add graceful curves to the flax by sliding the leaves between your thumb and the blunt edge of a knife.*

*Above: Chrysanthemums, the quintessential flowers of autumn, welcome the season the way no other flower can. This glorious profusion, in a riot of fall colors, features spray varieties with daisy, cushion, and anemone flower types. Eye-catching bicolor varieties add depth and vibrance. **Design Tip:** When grouping traditional fall colors like reds, yellows, and bronze, add an unexpected color, like the lavender used here, for a more sophisticated color story.*

Above: A distressed finish gives this wooden basket a rustic feel that complements its Asian style. Inside the basket, a mound of fall colored football mums is accented by sprigs of ivy for a glorious fall design. **Design Tip:** *While football mums are generally showcased individually, try gathering them together for a mounded look that really draws attention to their beautiful texture.*

Opposite page: Each level of this circular design's interplay not only presents a color shift but also a texture change, resulting in an energetic arrangement. Placing one variety against the next is a way to capture interest. **Design Tip:** *A random mixing of materials is not always necessary, nor must the florals all be displayed at one height. Try segregating them in rows for a contemporary look.*

A romantic and cherished flower, *Hydrangeas* were introduced to the west in the 1860s from Japan and China. The name *Hydrangea* is from the Greek words *hydro*, meaning water, and *aggos* for jar, which describes the cup-like shape of the fruits. *Hydrangea* symbolizes "Thank you for understanding" in the Victorian language of flowers.

Two species of *Hydrangeas* are commonly used as fresh and dried flowers: *Hydrangea macrophylla*, bigleaf or florist *Hydrangea*, and *Hydrangea paniculata*, panicle *Hydrangea*. The florist types are available as cut flowers and plants and are common flowering shrubs in the Southern states. The panicle types are hardier garden plants and are widely grown as "cut-your-own" landscape plants. The *Hydrangea* flower is a large cluster of four-petaled florets; the cluster shape may be rounded, broadly rounded, or the flat-topped lace cap variety. The lace cap types have sterile flower buds in the center and a pleasing ring of open flowers on the outside.

Hydrangeas have spectacular colors, including white, pink, purple, and blue. Forming an intriguing visual effect, pink and blue or other mixtures may both be present within the same flower cluster. Lace cap *Hydrangeas* are available in a wider range of colors including lavender, purple, rose, and mauve.

autumn hydrangeas

PHOTOGRAPHY BY STEPHEN SMITH

Hydrangeas form gorgeous single-flower designs as well as distinctive accents in combination with other flowers and foliages. *Hydrangeas* provide excellent mass, fullness, and emphasis. These old-fashioned, gardeny flowers suit a myriad of interiors and are equally beautiful used fresh, air-dried, or preserved. Use entire clusters in large showy designs with lilies and monkshood; trim portions of the cluster for creating impact in smaller designs.

Hydrangeas are available from January to October. At least half of the flowers should be open at purchase. Fresh cut *Hydrangeas* should display good color in the flowers and leaves; avoid buying stems with wilted blossoms or foliage. The stems should be recut and immediately placed into a warm vase solution for at least two hours before arranging. With proper care and handling, *Hydrangeas* will last five to ten days. Whether fresh-cut or potted, always keep the flowers well hydrated.

Hydrangeas may be dried both upside down or allowed to dry in a fresh design in a cool, dry, airy location. Air-dried *Hydrangeas* will appear beautifully papery and slightly wrinkled; preserved ones, treated with glycerin, will feel supple and bendable and may be dyed various colors. Dry environments, away from humidity and sunlight, will prolong their beauty and life.

At left: Whether used as a tasteful home accent or to enhance a special autumnal event, this gorgeous fresh Hydrangea wreath will not disappoint. It is perfectly suited for practically any purpose, from casual get-togethers to formal weddings. **Design Tip:** *Although cooler autumn temperatures help prevent wilting, these blossoms are thirsty, so arranging them in a wet foam wreath, as was done here, will prolong their beauty for hours of entertaining.*

Opposite page: One of today's most cherished floral materials, Hydrangeas form an exquisite single-flower design that can suit a wide variety of interiors. These naturally air-dried selections are arranged en masse for a striking, long-lasting decoration. **Design Tip:** *Hydrangeas are generally sold with short stems. To create a large arrangement like this, glue several pieces of foam together to create a column into which the short Hydrangea stems may be easily inserted.*

Dahlias are in their height of glory in the golden days of autumn. Dr. Anders Dahl, a Swedish botanist, first found diminutive *Dahlias* in Mexico in the late 1700s. The plant and its tubers were first valued as a vegetable, but that soon changed when new varieties with larger, double flowers were bred in Belgium in 1815. In the language of flowers, the Victorian meaning for *Dahlia* is instability.

Today's *Dahlias* are hybrids of two parents, *Dahlia coccinea* and *D. juarezii*. *Dahlias* are available in a wide range of sizes (two inches to ten inches across), shapes, textures, and colors. Some of the flower types include single, anemone, double, ball, pompon, semi-cactus, and cactus with narrow, pointed petals (ray flowers). These glamorous blossoms can be found in hues of white, cream, pink, yellow, peach, orange, red, lavender, purple, and bicolors. The foliage is a glossy dark green and is very attractive in arrangements.

Dahlias are dynamic in many styles of design, ranging from Oriental, formal, contemporary, or garden-style. The distinctive beauty of *Dahlias* adds mass to arrangements and provides emphasis and a focal area within a design. Some of the smaller types can be used as filler flowers. When designing with *Dahlias*, give the stems a fresh cut before placing the flowers in arrangements. Leaves may be left on the upper stems to give an attractive green framework to arrangements.

autumn dahlias

With unmatched beauty, *Dahlias* are in season from mid-summer through November. *Dahlias* should be picked or purchased before they are fully open for longer enjoyment indoors. Look for flowers with uniform color and undamaged blossoms. The leaves should not be yellowed. Recut the stems and immediately place them in a warm floral preservative solution. Remove any leaves that will be under water.

Depending on the type, *Dahlias* will last in vases or arrangements for two to ten days. Vase solution should be periodically changed. Position designs in cool, non-drafty places for maximum enjoyment of the flowers.

In autumn, an arrangement of *Dahlias* is truly a thing of beauty. The varieties of shapes and colors combine so beautifully with other seasonal flowers, foliages, berries, and fall accessories. *Dahlias* add pizazz as well as distinctive texture to any autumnal arrangement.

*Opposite page: Harvest time is wonderfully celebrated with this oblong basket arrangement. A bright red bed of vivid orange Dahlias creates excitement at the heart of the design while safflowers, Crocosmia, Hypericum, miniature persimmons, Setaria, oranges, Echinacea, and geranium leaves are draped over the basket's edges. **Design Tip:** Allow the Dahlias to shine in this arrangement by showcasing them at the center of the design. Place other natural materials around the Dahlias for textural interest.*

PHOTOGRAPHY BY MARK ROBBINS

*At right: Fiery Dahlias, juicy apples, and crisp fall leaves combine for a display full of autumn warmth and charm. Gathered casually in wooden baskets, these flowers are perfect for outdoor entertaining. **Design Tip:** Although the flowers convey the warmth of fall, they don't have to stand alone. Try adding baskets of apples, miniature pumpkins, or fall leaves to build a setting with the seasonal theme of harvest gathering.*

Halloween is a spooky and magical time for children of all ages. This autumn holiday is loaded with fun, like dressing up in costume, trick-or-treating, bobbing for apples, and carving jack-o'-lanterns. Costume parties are perfect opportunities for clever decorating with seasonal flowers and props. October 31 is Halloween, or All Hallow's Eve, an ancient celebration that combines aspects of Celtic autumn festivals with Christian customs, incorporated to downplay the pagan emphasis.

Historically, the most popular botanicals at Halloween are chrysanthemums, fall leaves, pumpkins, and gourds. Countless spooky accessories like spider webs, black cats, witches, and bats have been added to create animated designs. The most popular color scheme for Halloween is the combination of orange and black while accents of purple or lime green add a contemporary spark.

Suitable flowers for today's Halloween designs revolve around seasonal offerings. Popular chrysanthemums, along with yarrow, sunflowers, *Gladioli, Kalanchoe*, safflower, montbretia (*Crocosmia*), lilies, *Zinnias, Celosia*, carnations, and *Gerberas* can be used to create a fun Halloween arrangement. For a touch of green, add green 'Kermit' spray button mums, boxwood, or croton leaves; for a sprinkle of purple, try drumstick *Allium* or statice. Cattails, branches, vines, seeded *Eucalyptus*, cobra lilies, and dried materials add texture and a platform for adding spider webs, spiders, bats, and other spooky accessories. Fresh or permanent pumpkins, gourds, and miniature Indian corn add appropriate icons of the season to these for-fun-only creations.

autumn
halloween

For entertaining and decorating, Halloween accessories can be added to fall displays already in place. Designs with pumpkins placed in or near them, or designs in which the pumpkin is the container, are appropriate for the jack-o'-lantern holiday. For a bit of whimsy, add a spider web. Spider webs may be created with hot glue, string, or Spanish moss.

Halloween floral designs are great to bring out the kid in everyone! Casual designs featuring bats, black cats, and lively warm colors are enchanting additions to the Halloween festivities.

*At left: Cobwebs float from a barren vine that does double duty as the wooden container's faux handle. Lilies, Celosia, yarrow, and cattail spires comprise the design, which is guarded by a folk art sorceress. **Design Tip:** To create cobwebs, spray a flat piece of glass with cooking spray or aerosol plant shine. Then draw a web-shaped formation with the glue of a hot glue gun. When the glue is cool, gently peel the web away from the glass and attach it to the vine.*

*Opposite page: Perfect for window decorations or seasonal buffet tables, this gathering of lilies, carnations, miniature pumpkins, and other brightly colored materials is caught in the embrace of a smiling skeleton. Bare branches add height and Halloween flair. **Design Tip:** Use an animated figure to add whimsy to floral displays.*

PHOTOGRAPHY BY STEPHEN SMITH

Above: Fresh gladioli, carnations, and sunflowers provide a colorful forest-like setting for the home of nature's only flying nocturnal mammal. The novelty keepsake "bat house" is an enchanting Halloween-time version of a decorative birdhouse. Discarded sunflower stems create a pathway to the center of the design while fresh Leptospermum and boxwood, along with dried elm and preserved branches of oak leaves, enhance the woodland feeling. **Design Tip:** *Glue a novelty birdhouse into a round plastic plant tray. Add florals to create a visual "thicket" in the arrangement as well as a setting full of atmosphere.*

Opposite page: A Gothic bat-and-cobweb candelabra is at the center of an arrangement of fresh and permanent flowers. Long-lasting fresh boxwood and cut Kalanchoe look great with vibrant orange wood fiber ming roses, latex fruits, and oak leaves. **Design Tip:** *Eucalyptus seed branches can be spray-painted black to add a cobweb-like element to the mix.*

In autumn of 1621, William Bradford, the governor of Plymouth Colony and the leader of the pilgrims, declared a day of thanksgiving and prayer to celebrate the pilgrims' first harvest in the New World. Since that day, Thanksgiving has captured the essence of autumn with its rich warm colors and textures and its emphasis on the abundance of the harvest.

Traditionally, chrysanthemums, wheat, Indian corn, colorful fall leaves, fruits, and vegetables have been popular for Thanksgiving decorating. Fresh and dried plant materials in rich, warm colors are often mixed together with fresh florals to celebrate this bountiful holiday. The cornucopia, or horn of plenty, reigns with the turkey and the pilgrim as Thanksgiving's favorite icons.

autumn thanksgiving

The Thanksgiving holiday is perfect for celebrating the beautiful flowers and plant materials of autumn. Countless types of chrysanthemums, crested cockscombs (*Celosia*), orange fluffy safflowers, orange and yellow roses, carnations, *Gerberas*, *Dahlias*, sunflowers, montbretia (*Crocosmia*), yarrow, *Sedum*, pot marigolds (*Calendula*), and *Zinnias* are excellent autumnal flowers to choose for Thanksgiving centerpieces. The addition of berries such as *Hypericum*, rose hips, or *Sumac,* as well as materials such as wheat, oats, rye, cattails, autumn fruits and vegetables, along with beautiful fall foliage, makes the "abundance of the harvest" theme come alive.

The Thanksgiving meal would not be complete without flowers to add ambiance to the festive event. Centerpieces and vase arrangements in rich, warm autumnal colors complement the festivities well. The horn of plenty centerpiece so beautifully conveys the abundance of the harvest theme. Besides flowers, many materials are appropriate to add into designs or at the bases of designs to convey the abundance of a successful harvest. Featured materials might include gourds, miniature pumpkins, Indian corn, grains, grasses, nuts, fruits, vegetables, miniature straw bales, and colored leaves.

The Thanksgiving holiday welcomes generous helpings of beautiful plant materials, colorful fruits and vegetables, and eye-catching dried materials used in glorious abundance. Since the holiday centers on the dining experience, autumnal centerpieces and accessories are perfect to create the ambiance for giving thanks for a great harvest and for the blessings of family and friends.

*Opposite page: Vibrant, mossy green is a perfect background to showcase the glorious yield of a fall harvest. These colorful cornucopias are filled with myriad fall treats like rich brown lotus pods, robust pomegranates, pale rye sheaves, and luscious figs. **Design Tip:** Spray inexpensive rattan cornucopias with green paint and a layer of adhesive. Then place them in a bag with dried parsley flakes and shake to coat.*

*At right: With its fantail feather placement reminiscent of a proud Thanksgiving turkey, this holiday-inspired design will make a long-lasting arrangement following the feast. All of the materials, which include roses, California sage (Artemisia), saxicola (Thryptomene), and seeded Eucalyptus, will dry beautifully in place. The ivy is not likely to dry well and should be removed for best results. **Design Tip:** Roses, including both the miniature spray and standard tea used here, typically dry nicely, but designing them with short stems will yield the best results.*

A wedding in autumn can reflect the beauty of the season with the rich colors of the changing fall leaves. Autumn botanicals offer rich, vibrant colors and a variety of textures and shapes to enhance the ceremony and reception.

Early use of flowers at weddings is an English tradition. The simple nosegay, carried at social events, became the forerunner of today's wedding bouquet. The language of flowers gives the following meanings to autumn flowers and foliages: bittersweet, truth; chrysanthemum, cheerfulness; monkshood, chivalry; and wheat, friendliness or riches.

To create a lovely scene for an autumn wedding, many flowers and plant materials are available. Distinctive designs can be created using russet kangaroo paws, fluffy safflowers, Chinese lanterns, *Solidago*, chocolate-colored roses, and seasonal chrysanthemums. Rich, purplish-blue monkshood can be added for an accent color to larger altar or reception designs. Grasses, grains, and berries such as eye-catching bittersweet and mahogany *Hypericum* berries can be incorporated for a seasonal nod. Late summer garden flowers are still available and are very attractive for autumn weddings.

Many bouquet styles lend themselves well to autumn nuptials. An arm bouquet, a flowing hand-tied vertical grouping of flowers held along the bride's left forearm, is striking when created with seasonal flowers and accents. *Hydrangeas*, *Hypericum* berries, roses, goldenrod, sunflowers, and pheasant feathers combine for a pretty fall look. With their rich mixture of colors, *Hydrangeas* create classic monobotanical hand-tied bouquets. Keep *Hydrangeas* well watered and in vase solution until the bride marches down the aisle.

PHOTOGRAPHY BY NATHAN HAM

autumn weddings

Autumn weddings have ambiance all their own. The plant materials of this glorious season offer richly vibrant colors and pleasingly unique shapes and styles.

At left: Chosen to reflect the colorful beaded design on the gown and shawl, this grand oval bouquet features an adventurous gardeny combination of 'Skyline' roses, Dahlias, and Asclepias along with rose-scented geranium foliage, colorful coleus leaves, and tree of heaven foliage (Ailanthus). **Design Tip:** *When coordinating bouquets with intricately detailed attire, select flowers in colors and textures that match the patterns in the gowns, so the bouquets become extensions of the dresses.*

Opposite page: This collection of red and yellow roses and Hypericum berries and foliage is perfect for harvest-time weddings. Pheasant feathers strung on beading wire are wrapped around the bouquet's edge for a ruffly texture. **Design Tip:** *Create a matching choker—an organic option to jewelry—by twisting clusters of Hypericum berries and bunches of coffee foliage onto beading wire.*

Above: Through a cluster of Hydrangea blooms, this hand-tied arm bouquet is designed from the bottom up, with the stems of ascending florals arranged through previously placed blooms. Flowers include sunflowers, yarrow, goldenrod, feverfew, Limonium, and 'Sahara' roses. Imparting fall color are lavender pennyroyals and Hypericum berries. **Design Tip:** Add an autumn-inspired extension to the bouquet with pheasant feathers that are gently glued into the flower cluster.

Opposite page: Pairing such seemingly incompatible florals as dried star flowers and fresh Stephanotis blooms creates a dramatically modern bridal bouquet. **Design Tip:** Gather three bunches of dried star flowers and pat them gently into a dome shape. Trim the stems to create an even base. The ruffly edging of Stephanotises is achieved by gluing individual blossoms, on two-and-a-half-inch long wires, into the dome-shaped gathering of star flowers.

Autumn's unmatched beauty can be enjoyed from beginning to end with the vast selection of lifelike fabric flowers and permanent materials on the market today. From lavish arrangements for grand living spaces to miniature desktop accessories, permanent floral designs for fall offer something for everyone.

For the most realistic presentations, look for materials that have shapable stems and even shapable leaves. Also, look for those that are designed with slight imperfections in the blooms and foliage. Not only do the imperfections more closely imitate nature, they enhance the materials' lifelike beauty. Fall compositions of fabric florals and permanent botanicals would likely include a selection of items inspired by the season's bounty, but monobotanical arrangements of seasonal products are also appropriate. When working with only one material, look for those that have slight variations in color. Since the color in a fresh cut bunch of orange lillies, for example, varies slightly from flower to flower, so should the color of a grouping of fabric reproductions.

autumn everlastings

Especially for fall, permanent and dried materials can be combined with beautiful results, and fall offers a bounty of dried materials. The harvest season naturally leads to thoughts of gathering and collecting plant materials for autumn decorating and entertaining. Fall is brimming with possibilities for drying and preserving — colorful leaves, textural seed pods, unique gourds, graceful grasses, and an array of flowers.

Many materials can be dried and preserved for seasonal decorating and entertaining. Grasses, such as quaking grass (*Briza*), Northern sea oats, and pampas grass, along with grains, such as sorghum, broom corn, wheat, oats, hops, millet, and rye, can be harvested for a variety of textures. *Hydrangeas*, *Zinnias*, *Amaranthuses*, billy buttons (*Craspedia*), Chinese lanterns, *Sedum*, *Hypericum* berries, bittersweet, goldenrod, cattails, and button chrysanthemums all withstand the drying process well. Bear grass, teasel, and horsetail (*Equisetum*) also dry nicely. Cattails must be harvested very early in autumn (or late summer) to avoid shattering. Interesting seed pods can be purchased or collected along roadsides or from the garden.

Many plant materials are dried by being hung upside down; other materials will dry nicely upright. Grasses and seed heads with a pendulous nature will retain their graceful habit when supported upright in containers. The plant materials must have firm stems and be supported by tall containers during the drying process. Conditions must be cool, dry, well ventilated, and dark.

Opposite page: This topiary, in which sunflowers, Hydrangeas, and gourds are gathered around a floral foam sphere, will add lasting fall flair to any room of the house. A terra-cotta pot serves as the base, and its orange hue accents the color-turning gourds perfectly. **Design Tip:** *Topiaries generally have long trunks. For a modern look, and for the sake of visual variety, use a tall vase and a short trunk to vary the proportion.*

At right: Combining a myriad of gold and brown tones, this lush selection forms an elegant, long-lasting design. Featuring a delightful assortment of permanent gold roses, dried savanna sunflowers, and dried gourds, the wreath gets its fullness from bunches of preserved Southern oak leaves, which form a bed on which the other accents rest. **Design Tip:** *Tie bright yellow feathers on beading wire and weave the garland through the wreath to lend movement to an otherwise static design.*

PHOTOGRAPHY BY STEPHEN SMITH

159

Above: Clusters of hops provide the mechanics for this mixed arrangement of pomegranates and poppy pods accented by sesame bloom, sundrop yellow caviar, and stems of bittersweet. **Design Tip:** Use a combination of airy and ruffly materials against smooth and round materials for an interesting textural contrast.

Opposite page: A variety of warm-toned foliage, some berried, most variegated, takes center stage in this profusion of permanents. Playing a non-typical supporting role are the florals; a few stems of lisianthus and Delphinium are tucked deep into the composition. **Design Tip:** Gather weedy, ruffly materials together for an arrangement that focuses on mass of product rather than featuring focal blossoms.

Above: A quietly colorful composition with an almost neutral appearance, this wreath is a textural masterpiece of dried materials including seed balls, pomegranates, pine cone rosettes, cinnamon bundles, and assorted pods. Okra pods are arranged in a directional manner that gives rhythm to the design. **Design Tip:** Begin with a premade grapevine wreath and add materials in layers, pointing all linear additions in one direction to create a pattern of movement.

Opposite page: This modern topiary of feathers, dried pods, grasses, pine cones, and leaves is a stylish choice for today's homes. The striking display of natural materials rises above a simple, aged clay pot. **Design Tip:** To get gorgeous curves in pheasant feathers, run the feathers' ribs between your thumb and the blunt side of a knife until the desired curve is achieved.

Above: Silver paddle wire entwines grasses and grains including rye, wheat, barley, Phalaris, Linium, Avena, and Sarracenia. Pheasant feathers, sweet gum balls, and dried pomegranates are important textural additions. **Design Tip:** *Use wire to bind dried materials for a bale-like look that is perfect for fall. Then add preserved fruits, wedging them between the vertical placements of grasses.*

Opposite page: The chartreuse greens of fresh dock (Rumex) partner perfectly with the darker greens and rich browns in the myriad of preserved foliages found in this formally styled mass design. **Design Tip:** *Fresh dock will dry in place, which makes it a perfect accent for preserved foliages in a long-lasting creation.*

Above: Low, horizontal designs, among the most usable styles of all, allow every element to be showcased to the fullest. The varied assortment of materials provides a complex harmony of textures and colors. The fabric foliage is crafted to appear as naturally dried botanicals. **Design Tip:** For a credenza or dining table, long, low, flat designs like this basket creation add color without disrupting views of highlighted art or blocking eye contact during dinner.

Opposite page: A pair of coordinating arrangements, notable for their textural interplay and lack of form flowers, provide a relaxed wildflower influence to a formal setting. The hues of chartreuse, pink, and violet add playful yet sophisticated color to the formal antiques. **Design Tip:** Instead of a single large design, try creating two elevated spray designs for a classic, symmetry-in-decorating look.

winter
seasons of flowers

The brilliant white of winter snows and the joy and warmth of the holiday season guide winter floral designs. Amarylisses, stars of Bethlehem, paperwhites, orchids, and poinsettias are often available during this season.

For winter holidays, red and green are traditional color favorites. Add touches of silver, gold, and icy white or antique cream for a modern look. Evergreen clippings and pine cones also add festive touches to holiday designs. Holly and seasonal berries, especially deciduous holly, winterberry, and pepperberry, lend a holiday flair to winter arrangements.

When planning winter floral designs, who could forget Valentine's Day? While roses tend to be the most popular choice for this romantic day, tulips, Irises, carnations, and even exotic-looking orchids are excellent selections.

Above: White lisianthuses and tulips, along with pinkish-red Anemones, are casually arranged with Euphorbia marginata to create a Christmas centerpiece with a light new look. Metallic gold holly leaves add traditional elegance. **Design Tip:** Connect several vases together with berried branches to create a long centerpiece.

Opposite page: Classic holiday red and green are aptly displayed in this modern dome-shaped design. Red roses and Hypericum berries are tightly clustered in Biedermeier formation and set atop a sumptuous bed of greenery. A slender silver trumpet vase elevates the bouquet to star status. **Design Tip:** These flowers are arranged in the foam cage of a straight-handled bouquet holder. The handle then slips easily into a vase.

Opposite page: Here, the traditional cone shape associated with the winter holiday season is re-created with some unexpected materials. Roses, dusty miller (Senecio), and variegated Pittosporum combine beautifully for a Christmas tree that is modern and eye-catching. **Design Tip:** To create a base for your tree, stack several pieces of floral foam together and then slice them into a cone shape. Reinforce the foam with wooden picks.

Above: Arranged in a foam wreath form, this all-white centerpiece is beautifully enhanced by pastel pink and silver ornaments placed decoratively into the center of the foam form. With the incorporation of the wreath, a seasonal icon, this elegant creation is wonderful for holiday tables. **Design Tip:** Arrange the flowers in the foam wreath form first. Then fill the center of the wreath with a mass of fabulous ornaments that echo the monochromatic beauty of the florals.

173

Amaryllises are elegant flowers for the winter holidays. Their beauty is bold, eye-catching, and long lasting as both cut flowers and blooming plants. Amaryllis, or *Hippeastrum*, is native to the tropical regions of the world. The flower is named for a Greek shepherdess in the Roman poet Vergil's Eclogues. Another common name for amaryllis is Barbados lily. In the language of flowers, bold amaryllis blossoms mean pride, timidity, or splendid beauty.

Amaryllises are available with single, double, or miniature flowers. The distinctive, trumpet-shaped flowers are borne in a whorl at the top of a long leafless stem. Colors available include white, red, pink, salmon, peach, orange, greenish-yellow, and bicolors.

winter
amaryllises

PHOTOGRAPHY BY STEPHEN SMITH

Contemporary designs are well-suited for amaryllises because of their attention-getting shape, lengthy stems, and color selection. Of course, a blooming amaryllis plant is a long-lasting Christmas gift or decorative item. Amaryllises may also be great additions to traditional centerpieces, mantel pieces, or entryway designs. The amaryllis adds accent and a focusing emphasis to any design. Monochromatic masses are elegant and dramatic in vase arrangements. For another contemporary vase design, the showy flowers can be combined with touches of winterberry holly and white pine in a sleek metal container.

Additional support for the top-heavy amaryllis stems can be achieved by inserting a wooden stake or piece of bamboo into the hollow stem before placing amaryllises into designs. To design with amaryllises in floral foam, insert wooden stakes into the hollow stems, allowing the stakes to extend beyond the stem end. Invert the stem and fill the hollow area with water, adding a wad of cotton at the stem opening to plug it. Wrap the stem end with waterproof tape to secure the cotton and prevent the stem from splitting. Gently insert the stake and stem into wet floral foam.

Amaryllises are now available year-round with peak supply from October to March. The cut flower or plant should be purchased in the bud stage. Buds should be expanding and just showing color. The flower stalk will be attractive for one to two weeks because individual florets will continue to develop and open as the older florets fade. Recut the stems and place them in a floral preservative solution to keep bacteria from growing in the water. The stem ends may split and curl, but this condition does not shorten the flower life. Periodically recut the curled ends.

*At left: Fresh pears sprayed with brilliant gold paint give this mounded composition, featuring amaryllises, incense cedar, and Oregonia, true holiday elegance. The pots have been painted to coordinate with the gilded fruit. **Design Tip:** The paint treatment is far more economical than purchasing artificial fruit, and it's workable for party use because painted fruit will last about one week.*

*Opposite page: A perfect accent to today's minimalist décor, these amaryllis blossoms in sleek aluminum vases are full of seasonal charm. The effort is minimal, too. Simply fill the vases with water and flower food, then drop in a few beautiful blooms. **Design Tip:** Arrange amaryllises in a series of vases so that the blossoms can be showcased without overcrowding.*

Opposite page: These stunning amaryllis blossoms are beautifully showcased in a vertical arrangement. The quintessential winter flowers, amaryllises don't need much dressing up to add glamour to holiday affairs.
Design Tip: *Bunchings of bear grass, wedged into the vase in an oval shape, provide an attractive support apparatus for the massive flower stems.*

Above: A single amaryllis bulb in a clay pot makes an exquisite holiday gift requiring no additional adornments. To quickly dress up a room with understated holiday elegance, try a row of amaryllises in sleek containers.
Design Tip: *When giving a potted plant as a gift, it's important that the plant is placed in an attractive container and that the soil is covered with interesting mosses or pebbles.*

The carnation lends its cheerful color and light scent to brighten wintry days. Carnations originated in Europe and Asia and have a long history of use as garden flowers and cut flowers for arrangements. Although carnations generally mean "fascination," different sentiments can be conveyed by using various colors of carnations. White carnations symbolize innocence; pink ones say "I'll never forget you." Red means "My heart aches for you" while striped ones mean "Sorry I can't be with you." Not all meanings are positive; yellow carnations stand for disdain and purple ones for capriciousness.

winter carnations

Carnations, *Dianthus caroyphyllus*, range in flower size, number of blossoms per stem, and color. Standard or full-size carnations have one flower per stem and are the largest of all carnations. Miniature carnations have multiple smaller flowers per stem. Chinese miniature carnations are small-flowered, nonbranching types with one or two flowers per stem. The single-petaled type of carnation, called Gipsy bloom, exhibits multiple dainty flowers on branched stems. The color range includes every color except blue and bicolors. Blue carnations are in the development stage but currently appear mauve, violet, or lavender. Sweet William, *Dianthus barbatus*, is a related flower with a clustered head of multiple flowers.

From formal centerpieces to casual vase arrangements, carnations are well adapted to many floral design styles and uses. Design styles include mounded Biedermeier arrangements, garden, and pavé as well as corsages, boutonnieres, and wedding bouquets. Carnation and miniature carnations add mass, filler, and accent to designs.

The colorful, long-lasting carnation is available year-round. They can be purchased in the bud stage and will open well with proper care. Miniature carnations should have at least one open flower on the stem. Avoid purchasing any carnation that has a split calyx, the green outer covering around the lower part of the petals. Each carnation flower head should be firm and should spring back when touched. Soft flower heads, or "sleepy" carnations, should be avoided.

After purchasing, recut the stems and place them in warm floral preservative solution. Avoid ethylene exposure because it causes "sleepiness" in carnations. Ethylene sources to avoid include fruit, decaying flowers and foliage, and exhaust. Carnations' vase life can be one to two weeks or longer.

Opposite page: A finely detailed silver candle holder is surrounded by rings of ruffly red carnations in this timeless holiday centerpiece. A deep red candle, embraced by the upper ring of carnations, echoes the warm feelings at holiday gatherings. **Design Tip:** *Place a floral foam wreath around the base of a candleholder. Add another piece of foam at the candleholder's top and cut it to form a ring that will embrace the candle. Fill the rings with carnations in pavé fashion.*

Above: A glorious profusion of magnificent red carnations is massed into a beautiful bundle and placed in a softly hued vase. A lavender ribbon stylishly accents the design. **Design Tip:** *For an easy-to-make design, cluster a bunch of carnations to resemble a single oversized flower. Drop the gathering into a clear vase.*

Opposite page: The unusual 'Tropic Butterfly' carnation, with its captivating appearance, is a wonderful flower for vase arrangements. In addition to its butterfly-shaped petal formation, its delicate clove fragrance is sure to please. **Design Tip:** *Spray carnations benefit from monobotanical placements, which allow the remarkable blossoms to shine.*

Above: Foil-lined paper planters sporting a weathered finish are the ideal beginning to these carnation creations arranged in pavé fashion. **Design Tip:** *Try using like containers and showing off different color varieties of the same flower. The contrast makes for a pleasantly off-beat display.*

Orchids are beloved flowers for any occasion. These exquisite flowers are particularly well loved at Christmas and Valentine's Day as cut flowers or plants. Orchids were first found growing abundantly in tropical areas. Although highly prized for centuries, orchids became more popular and widely grown since the 1920s due to an improved method of seed germination. In the Victorian language of flowers, orchids mean "You are beautiful."

Exotic orchids are numerous, with thousands of species or types. While varying in size, shape, and coloration, orchids have a distinctive lower petal, called a lip, that is very different from the other petals. Many of the orchids are available as sprays, which have multiple flowers on one stem. As cut flowers, some important ones include *Cattleya*, *Cymbidium*, *Dendrobium*, *Oncidium*, *Paphiopedilum*, *Phalaeonopsis*, and *Vanda*. No common names are associated with many types of orchids; instead, most are simply referred to by their scientific names.

winter orchids

PHOTOGRAPHY BY STEPHEN SMITH

The *Cattleya* orchid was named for William Cattley in the early 1800s and is available in white, pink, lavender, and yellow. The hollow lip of the *Cymbidium* orchid inspired its name, which comes from for the Greek word, *kymbe*, for boat. *Cymbidiums* have the widest range of color and are available in white, pink, peach, red, purple, yellow, green, brown, and bicolors. *Dendrobiums* are named for the Greek words meaning tree and life, which refer to their growth in trees in their native habitat. These orchids are white, yellow, pink, lavender, purple, green, and bicolors. The yellow *Oncidium* orchid is named from the Greek word for tumor because of the flower's swelled lower lip. *Oncidiums* have a characteristic flecking of orange, red, or brown on some of the petals. The common name for *Paphiopedilum* is lady's slipper orchid, from the Greek word *pedilon* meaning slipper. The lady's slipper orchid is borne singly in purple, green, and bicolors. Since *Phalaeonopsis* means "resembling a moth" in Greek, another common name is the moth orchid. Moth orchids are white, lavender, or yellow. Fragrant *Vanda* orchids have a wide variety of colors with spotted patterns.

Popular orchids have year-round availability. Look for flowers with uniform color. The flowers should not be browned, wilted, or translucent (from cold injury). Purchase *Oncidium* orchids when the buds are just beginning to open. When buying by the stem, one or two flowers should be open. *Dendrobium* sprays should have one-third of the flowers open. Place the flowers in floral preservative solution. Avoid ethylene exposure and cool temperatures below 50° F. Orchids are very long lasting. *Cattleya* orchids last seven to ten days while the other types may last two weeks or longer.

*Opposite page: This luxuriously massed arrangement underlines the fact that simplicity is king when working with cut orchids. Adding too much crowds their stately beauty. **Design Tip:** When arranging large sprays of orchids, excess foliage can detract from, or even cover up, the beauty of the blossoms.*

*At left: These spectacular orchids derive their common name, lady's slipper, from the unique shape of their lip, which forms a pocket. In this simple design, three exotic blooms are stunningly presented in a pared-down manner. **Design Tip:** Provide detailed attention for these beauties by combining tufts of moss, clusters of seeded Eucalyptus, and a few Ruscus leaves at the base of the faux-planted design.*

Opposite page: Featuring several different genera of orchids, including Dendrobium, Oncidium, and Phalaenopsis, this collection showcases the graceful beauty of flower-filled orchid stems. Dropped into several styles of gilded pots, these exotic flowers are ready to decorate for the holidays. **Design Tip:** A collection of containers in different shapes and sizes can add to the beauty of a holiday presentation. The gilded treatment unites the grouping of pots.

Above: The essence of elegance, this stem of white Phalaenopsis orchid blossoms stands majestically on its own, with little ornamentation required. Only a pot befitting the orchid's beauty need be added. **Design Tip:** Give potted orchids special treatment by transferring them to gorgeous containers that suit their royal image.

185

winter poinsettias

The poinsettia is the beautiful, brilliantly colorful symbol of Christmas. First cultivated by the Aztecs in ancient Mexico, this flower has a long history. Poinsettias were first discovered in Mexico when Joel R. Poinsett, the first U.S. minister to Mexico in 1825, brought the flower back to the United States. The brilliant red flower was renamed for him.

Poinsettias, *Euphorbia pulcherrima*, are available as single, double, or curled bract types. The actual flowers of poinsettias are small and located in the center. The showy red "petals" are actually leaf-like bracts. The color range is red, pink (light, medium, and hot), cream, and yellow with bracts that are solid, mottled, or flecked. The development of a rose-violet color is a future goal. Some poinsettias may have variegated foliage, showing white, green, and yellow-green coloration. Flowers related to the poinsettia are arching spurge, *Euphorbia fulgens*, and variegated snow-on-the-mountain, *Euphorbia marginata*.

Poinsettias are extremely popular blooming plants at Christmas. Some plants are trained as "tree" poinsettias and are beautiful massed with shorter varieties in front of them. The pots may be decorated with foil or placed in lined baskets or decorative containers. The addition of white pine or branches adds texture and line. Before displaying, position the bracts prominently above the green leaves for showier presentations.

Poinsettias may also be used as cut flowers for accent and emphasis in festive winter or Christmas floral designs. The showy flowers may be used singly in vases, massed in monobotanical formation in vases and arrangements, or combined with other flowers in centerpieces. For a simple but eye-catching centerpiece, cluster small vases in the center of a table, each with a small, curled poinsettia bloom in it. Although vase solutions are preferable, well-conditioned poinsettias can be arranged in foam.

Poinsettias are available from November to January. Look for bracts with uniform color and well-formed shape. The small yellow flowers should just be starting to appear in the center. The leaves should be uniform in color and shape and not excessively yellow or rolled.

Poinsettias, and all *Euphorbia,* will exude a milky sap when the stem is cut or the leaves are removed. To condition the cut flower properly and avoid immediate wilting, place the freshly cut stem ends in hot water treated with a floral preservative. The milky sap may cause an allergic skin reaction in some persons. The vase life of a poinsettia is seven to nine days.

PHOTOGRAPHY BY MARK ROBBINS

The pungent fragrance of evergreens brings thoughts of Christmas to mind. Evergreen boughs or fresh Christmas trees enliven rooms with the aromas of Christmases past. During the Middle Ages, the Germans first brought live evergreen trees into their homes to celebrate Christmas. They believed that evergreens or conifers had protective powers because they "stayed alive" during the winter months.

Evergreens may be needle bearing, like conifers (cone bearing) or broadleaf, such as boxwood and holly. Conifers include fir (*Abies*), spruce (*Picea*), pine (*Pinus*), arborvitae (*Thuja*), juniper (*Juniperus*), and cedar (*Cedrus*). Some examples of the aromatic firs are noble fir, silver fir, and balsam fir. Douglas fir (*Pseudotsuga*) is another closely related evergreen with attractive short needles. Several types of spruce, juniper, arborvitae, white and ponderosa pine, and atlas and deodar cedar are attractive and fragrant evergreens for Christmas decorating. The evergreen cones are also attractive for Christmas displays or designs. Hemlock (*Tsuga*) is not commonly used because of needle drop. English holly (*Ilex aquifolium*) is a beloved plant material for Christmas decorating. Both the green and variegated types, with their colorful red berries, are popular. Boxwood (*Buxus*) is a broadleaf evergreen with small attractive leaves.

winter
evergreens

Fresh evergreens are seasonally available in November and December. A great source for leftover evergreen boughs are Christmas tree lots because they remove the lower branches when fitting the trees for stands. Evergreens should exhibit fresh color with no browning on the newer growth. In cool environments away from sunlight, conifers are very long lasting. Although the needles eventually dry out, the color is very natural looking for four to six weeks or longer. Holly and boxwood should be recut, placed into preservative solution, and kept in a cool spot. Holly arrangements will last two to three weeks if well watered. Boxwood designs or Christmas trees will dry lighter green and last indefinitely.

At left: Whether in a beach house or the home of one who loves the sea, this mantel design, featuring starfish, urchins, and shells, would surely delight the owner. Selected for its resemblance to both aquatic plants and traditional evergreens, Australian pine is laid atop the mantel and is accented by a nautical cotton sailcloth ribbon. Shiny gold and iridescent ornaments add a touch of traditional Christmas to the sea-inspired décor. **Design Tip:** *When placing evergreens directly onto a mantel or other furnishing, seal off the ends of the stems with glue or stem wrap, so sap doesn't seep onto the mantel.*

Opposite page: A lavish mix of holiday greens, arranged in a stately bronze urn, is accented by oranges and pomanders in this inventive creation that exudes the fragrances of the yuletide season. A silver platter at the arrangement's base holds more oranges and pomanders, which are entwined by a glorious garland of greens. **Design Tip:** *When working with seasonal greens, save the tips. Using thin-gauge paddle wire, connect them together in garland fashion for a wonderful tabletop accessory.*

winter
christmas

'Tis the season of joy and wonder and of gathering with family to share gifts near the Christmas tree. Christmas carols, candlelight, poinsettias, ornaments, tinsel, and fresh evergreen scent lace the holiday with wonderful sights, smells, and sounds. Christmas commemorates the birth of Jesus Christ and is celebrated on December 25. A Roman calendar first listed Christmas in 336 A.D. By 1100, Christmas was the most important religious holiday in Europe.

Germans and other Europeans first brought fresh trees into their homes. The original Christmas trees were small, tabletop sized, and decorated with presents. In European countries, St. Nicholas became the symbol of the holiday. The Santa Claus figure developed from this early gift giver. Wreaths, symbolizing eternal life, became popular to decorate homes as did the yule log, a tradition from Scandinavian countries, France, and Great Britain.

Berry-filled branches of holly and evergreens such as pine, spruce, arborvitae, fir, cedar, boxwood, Italian *Ruscus*, *Eucalyptus*, and lots of textural cones set the backdrop for beautiful Christmas floral designs. Cut poinsettias, roses, orchids, and lilies remain popular although many more new favorites are perfect for the holidays as well. Amaryllises, *Alstroemerias*, *Anemones*, and *Gerberas* lend a contemporary flair. Poinsettia plants continue to be popular.

Today's Christmas decorating begins with the Christmas tree and expands to nearly every room in the house. The Christmas tree may be glorious in traditional colors and baubles but can express many styles, including a garden feel with dried flower bunches resting in the branches. Harkening back to earlier times, small tabletop topiaries make a sophisticated statement. Centerpieces and floral designs for the dining room table, buffet, counter, or desk add the fresh scent of pine and the glint of gold from ribbon and ornaments. Garlands may decorate windows, doorways, stairway banisters, or may be suspended as statements all their own. Wreaths are beautifully varied, including the abundantly fruited della Robbia style.

The Christmas season is inviting and compelling in its celebration of spiritual and family traditions. Flowers and fresh evergreens add beauty and charm to every aspect of the holiday.

Opposite page: Glossy green Magnolia leaves are accented by lush apples and brilliant red roses for a memorable holiday arrangement. Clustered in a formal silver urn, these vividly colored botanicals celebrate the joy of the holiday season. **Design Tip:** *For dramatic flair, gather roses and apples into tightly massed sections, then arrange the leaves so they burst out between the groupings.*

Above: Two gorgeous holiday decoratives, composed of vibrant red roses, sprigs of fresh pine, and permanent holly, are created with the addition of tall tree topper ornaments, which extend the visual emphasis of stately silver vases. **Design Tip:** The tree toppers are supported by leftover taper candles, which have been inserted into the foam that fills the containers.

Opposite page: Greet winter visitors with a stunning door wreath that overflows with sumptuous colors and textures. Permanent roses, faux berries, holiday ornaments, evergreens, and vines in all of the rich hues of the season are embraced by a gorgeous satiny bow. **Design Tip:** Use an organza table runner to create a wide, dramatic bow befitting the size and impact of the wreath.

Opposite page: Highlighted by the twinkling lights of pillar candles and European oil lamp candles, coordinating arrangements of permanent berries, berried branches, and foliage celebrate the richness of the holiday season. **Design Tip:** Use plates of candles to extend centerpieces.

Above: A stunning assortment of Czechoslovakian blown glass ornaments makes a stylish holiday presentation. Better yet, this gorgeous centerpiece takes only minutes to arrange. **Design Tip:** Use a bowl of ornaments for modern holiday flair and arrange them in the manner that one might arrange traditional fruits, pine cones, or evergreens.

Above: *A gathering of Pyracantha berries and sprengeri fern cascade in glorious holiday fashion from the center of this design, which features permanent and beaded pomegranates, ornaments, and a twig sphere.* **Design Tip:** *When displaying berries and grasses in a tall container, add a long piece of satin ribbon, draped over the side, to accentuate the container's height.*

Opposite page: Perfect for a door hanging or for display on holiday tables, this lush wreath is an exquisite feast for the eyes. Roses, evergreens, faux fruits, and ornaments create a warm welcome. **Design Tip:** *Add fresh roses in water picks to a wreath for a special event. Allow the roses to dry in place for a longer lasting design.*

*Opposite page: An almost complementary color combination imparts a modern and somewhat Southern vibrancy to this nontraditional, designer-made tree. The composition of materials includes satin-finish glass ornaments, miniature fruits, and permanent flowers. **Design Tip:** Finishing touches make this design memorable. An inverted silver tussie mussie holder completes the tree's top while a butterfly graces the side.*

*Above: Gorgeous translucent Christmas ornaments, in trendy iridescent hues, expand the range of holiday colors and add a shimmery luster to seasonal décor. **Design Tip:** Filling clear glass globe vases with ornaments creates a simple but dramatic holiday display.*

Opposite page: A traditional evergreen wreath is composed with an assortment of seasonal elements, both modern and old-fashioned. Clove-studded oranges, clusters of berries, apples, oranges, and ornaments reminiscent of Christmas past are all set off by a crisp red tie of ribbon. **Design Tip:** Combining old-fashioned looking ornaments with fruits creates a fresh take on the classic della Robbia look.

Above: Inspired by the traditional, heavily fruited style of Colonial Williamsburg, this beautifully abundant wreath features a collection of today's most realistic permanent fruits. The addition of permanent amaryllis blossoms and foliage, along with dried pomegranates and leaves, gives this artificial wreath design a thoroughly modern update. **Design Tip:** Shape the long, narrow amaryllis leaves so they entwine some of the fruits, resulting in a woven effect.

Above: Arranged in a bow-shaped, rusted iron candleholder, these gilded fruits, nuts, and leaves are a woodsy, nature-inspired composition. Alone or in multiples, this single-candle centerpiece is suited for a rustic setting. *Design Tip:* A pillar candle makes a great focal point for small holiday decorations. Simple but elegant ribbon adds contrast.

Opposite page: A natural trans-seasonal holiday design features permanent berries and preserved cedar as well as fresh ti tree that will dry in place. Along with a premade topiary of Sequoia cones, a trio of seagrass-and-wood angels, a pecan garland, and weathered candlesticks all complement the natural woodland theme. *Design Tip:* Detail the tabletop around an arrangement with coordinating pieces that expand on the overall theme.

Above: A rustic wire urn is a natural displayer for a modern gathering of ornaments, greenery, and a faux bird's nest. **Design Tip:** Celebrate the mix. Christmastime is a great opportunity to combine exquisitely crafted ornaments with elements gathered from nature.

Opposite page: Permanent conical topiaries, representative of traditional Christmas greens, portray the well manicured shrubs seen in many formal gardens. For the holidays, they make sophisticated statements when left unadorned yet are gloriously enhanced with a wreath of preserved roses and other permanent flowers, foliages, and dried tallow berries that is planted around the base. **Design Tip:** For a simple and stylish holiday look, top urns with permanent cones of faux foliage.

Above: A low arrangement of freeze-dried pomegranates, crab apples, and cabbage roses serves as an elegant candleholder and centerpiece. ***Design Tip:*** *Nestle a pillar candle inside an urn and arrange flowers around it. Use a candle that is tall enough so that the floral materials will not be too near the open flame.*

Opposite page: Candles are a Christmas standard, and a variety of Asian-inspired metal holders, including pewter-washed hanging metal lanterns and wire screen votive holders, illuminate this Oriental setting. Faux peonies and permanent pomegranates, both natives of Asia, fit perfectly into this theme. Glass ornaments with Chinese characters complete the look. ***Design Tip:*** *Use collections of elements to augment floral displays. Here, Asian lanterns enhance the setting, but practically any item, including seasonal vases, candles, and Santa figurines or other collectibles, could be used.*

The loveliness of a beaming bride and groom at the Christmas season is a joy to behold. Fragrant evergreens and rich floral colors add to the romance and beauty of the ceremony. Compared to the outdoor landscape, winter weddings allow the flowers and plant materials to be center stage.

The English are credited with fashioning the first wedding bouquets. During the Victorian era, individual flowers and foliages were assigned a symbolic meaning to allow the bride to convey her thoughts about the day and her husband-to-be. Some flowers and foliages had the following meanings: white carnation, remember me; holly, domestic happiness; orchid, you are beautiful; lavender heather, admiration; and calla, magnificent beauty.

Winter plant materials include amaryllises, orchids, carnations, poinsettias, scarlet plume (*Euphorbia fulgens*), heather, holly, winterberry, pepperberry, and evergreens of all kinds. Roses, callas, and feathery chrysanthemums also find their way into winter wedding designs. Decorated Christmas trees and cones are unique to the winter wedding look.

Winter bouquets encompass a variety of color schemes and styles. Winter white is a classic look while red makes a dramatic seasonal statement. Traditional, contemporary, and stylized bouquet selections give each bride a tremendous choice to suit her personality.

Winter bouquets incorporate red more than bouquets in any other season. Red roses are a classic; however, holly with red berries, pepperberries and red carnations, spray mums, or miniature poinsettias also fill the need for Christmas-like red. With the popularity of round bouquets, a red duchess rose bouquet is a unique stylized design to achieve a wintry round look. The duchess rose bouquet is a composite design, created by adding rose petals around a single rose until the fuller round shape is reached. Leaves around the edge support the petals and finish the back of the bouquet.

winter
weddings

The winter wedding brings together beautiful flowers with the textural variety of fragrant evergreens, foliages, cones, and berries. The winter landscape gives a poignant beauty to the radiant bride and her wedding flowers.

Opposite page: In peak supply from December through March, snowballs (Viburnum) are ideal for creating stylish monobotanical bouquets. And they're simple to construct, whether hand-tied or arranged in a bouquet holder. **Design Tip:** *Woody-stemmed snowballs need plenty of water to prevent wilting, so making the bouquet in a foam holder or leaving a hand-tied bouquet in a vase of water until the last minute is advisable.*

At right: Providing a distinctive alternative to the lace or leaf collars that often encircle bridal bouquets, feathery plumes of fresh Astilbe radiate from the base of this lush composition of spray roses, lisianthuses, and Bouvardia. A true classic, this bouquet can be hand-tied or designed in a bouquet holder. **Design Tip:** *Use a spiky flower like Astilbe to create a striking edging for a wedding bouquet.*

PHOTOGRAPHY BY MARK ROBBINS

Opposite page: A bold, daring alternative to traditional bridal bouquets, this feathery boa, created from vivid red carnations, is sure to grab attention. **Design Tip:** To construct a carnation boa, remove the stems close to the flowers' bases. Then thread the flower heads onto a thin wire, monofilament, or florist twine, hiding the green calyx of the flower in the petals of the next threaded flower.

Above: A popular color choice of many winter brides, red can make a dramatic seasonal statement. This hand-tied, Biedermeier style nosegay features a collar of fluffy carnations encircling a cluster of Bupleurum and miniature pine cones. **Design Tip:** To achieve the look shown here, trim the Bupleurum into a smooth dome, then glue miniature pine cones into place.

PHOTOGRAPHY BY NATHAN HAM

Opposite page: Shiny glass Christmas ornaments make a festive statement in this bridal bouquet. Red roses, statice, and many varieties of foliage combine in this glorious seasonal gathering. **Design Tip:** To add instant seasonal charm, dress up bouquets with small ornaments and gold corsage leaves.

Above: These gorgeous red roses have an extravagant, velvety appearance when assembled in a composite design. A collar of gilded leaves gives the bouquet an opulent feel and lends support to the delicate petals. **Design Tip:** Wire two rose petals at a time with thin, hairpin-shaped wires. Twist the wires at the base of the clusters. Tape the clusters around a single rose head until the desired fullness is achieved.

Valentine's Day and romance go together. February 14 is the day to express love and affection. Cupids, hearts, and red roses all convey love and tenderness for that special someone. Although the exact origin of Valentine's Day is uncertain, a popular belief is that an early Christian saint named Valentine befriended the children of his village. However, Saint Valentine refused to worship the Roman gods and was thrown in jail. All of the children missed him and wrote messages to him, tossing these notes to him through the bars of his cell window. The giving of colorful Valentine's Day cards and gifts was, according to the legend, based on this event.

winter
valentine's day

PHOTOGRAPHY BY STEPHEN SMITH

In the late 1800s and early 1900s, the favored floral gifts for Valentine's Day were violets. Corsage bouquets of violets were the most popular gift for loved ones. To make corsage bouquets, violets were fashioned into bunches of 100 to 300 with another flower such as gardenia or lily-of-the-valley placed in the center of the bunch of violets. To complete the design, a backing of foliage was added. Roses soon became popular Valentine's Day gifts. Other historically popular flowers include lilies-of-the-valley, orchids, sweet peas, carnations, and spring bulbs.

The Valentine's Day flowers for today's sweethearts revolve around red flowers, particularly red roses, but a large variety of colors and flowers are suitable for the romantic day. Pink, burgundy, rose, white, purple, and blue are other great Valentine's Day colors. Spring flowers such as tulips, *Irises*, *Anemones*, daffodils, stocks, and sweet peas continue to be popular. *Alstroemerias*, *Anthuriums*, *Astilbe*, baby's breath, *Boronia*, drumstick *Alliums*, *Freesias*, *Genista*, *Gerberas*, heather, larkspurs, *Nerine* lilies, Queen Anne's lace, and waxflowers are lovely, multi-colored additions to Valentine's Day floral designs.

Vases of long-stemmed roses remain the symbol of love for many at Valentine's Day. Mixed bouquets with spring flowers and fillers are also fitting to express love and affection. A vase arrangement of tulips, roses, and hyacinths is just the right combination.

At left: This monochromatic aster arrangement features several special touches that any recipient will enjoy. A sheer fabric envelopes the clear glass vase, and a tie-on handmade paper heart beautifully accents the gathering. The paper heart is filled with seeds for later planting. **Design Tip:** *Cover a clear vase with tulle, organza, or silk fabric for a romantic, dressed-up look.*

Oppposite page: This glorious, gardeny combination will warm any heart on Valentine's Day. Tulips, roses, and carnations, in pretty hues from brilliant red to soft pink, spill out from a clear glass vase. **Design Tip:** *For a natural accessory, cut heart shapes out of moss. The hearts can be decorated with pansies or left unadorned.*

214

PHOTOGRAPHY BY STEPHEN SMITH

Above: Rising from gilded pots in a burst of waxflower and other filler flowers, these arrangements resemble garden wonderments far more than simple potted plants. **Design Tip:** *Create a topiary-like trunk by surrounding a cylinder vase with discarded rose stems. Bind the stems with metallic wire and "plant" the entire trunk in a clay pot. Then simply drop the desired flowers into the vase to complete the attractive creations.*

Opposite page: The time-honored gift of red roses receives an update in this stylish bouquet. Classic red is mixed with blush roses, stocks, and tufts of baby's breath for a modern look. **Design Tip:** *All-red roses for Valentine's Day can be made more exciting if augmented with a little variety. Try mixing in new colors or textures to add interest.*

Above: Fabulous gifts for garden lovers, these topiary-style gatherings of carnations appear to be planted in painted, moss-topped pots. Quickly accented by craft store wooden hearts, these easily assembled designs are a sweet choice for the holiday of love. **Design Tip:** Adding geranium foliage to your creations lends a citrus scent and a fresh color contrast that recipients will treasure.

Opposite page: Bearing this mixed floral presentation, these terra-cotta cherubs present a compact design featuring roses, lilies, and Alstroemeria. **Design Tip:** Look for inexpensive cherubs, hearts, or other romantic-themed gifts to add animation to your Valentine's Day designs.

218

Above: In complementary peach and blue, this delightful design is created in a wonderful copper basket with a raffia tassel. The premium blooms and elegant basket enhance the value for Valentine's Day. **Design Tip:** No one wants to skimp on Valentine's Day, so even with smaller-sized arrangements, opt for premium blooms for fabulous presentations.

Opposite page: Eye-catching hot pink is the focus of this decidedly feminine design. Carnations, roses, statice, and heather in bright, hot hues will win any valentine's heart. **Design Tip:** Photocopied love poems attached to painted pots with the help of spray adhesive add a literary flair to Valentine's Day sentiments.

O, my luve is like a red, red rose
That's newly sprung in June:
O, my luve is like a melodie
That's sweetly play'd in tune.

Robert Burns

Roses are red,
violets are blue,
sugar is sweet,
and so are you.

There is a garden
in her face where roses
and white lilies blow;
the heavenly paradise is
that place, wherein all
pleasant fruits do flow.

Thomas Campion

Opposite page: This basket arrangement overflows with a collection of beautiful blossoms. Roses, Gerberas, carnations, and waxflowers burst from a bed of ivy in this gardeny design. **Design Tip:** *Cover basket handles with graceful bows of pink wired ribbon to add personality to the design and customize the container.*

Above: This fragrant, hand-tied nosegay rests in a heart-shaped papier-mâché box, the sides of which have been adorned with salal leaves protected with clear glaze. **Design Tip:** *Nestle a nosegay into a paper box to create a romantic gift presentation.*

Floral Design by Talmage McLaurin.

Text by Dianne Noland.

Photography by Stephen Smith, Mark Robbins, Ash Youssef, Nathan Ham, Kate Wootton, and Maxine Jacobs.

Published by Florist Review Enterprises.

Captions and Copy Editing by Heather Corley, Shelley Urban, and David Coake.

Design and Typesetting by Kate Wootton, Ana Maben, Stacey Wyant; Artemis, Topeka, Kansas.

Printed in the United States by The John Henry Company, Lansing, Michigan.

Separations and Postscript services by Capital Graphics, Inc., Topeka, Kansas.

ISBN 0-9654149-8-1 (hardcover)

ISBN 0-9654149-9-X (softcover)

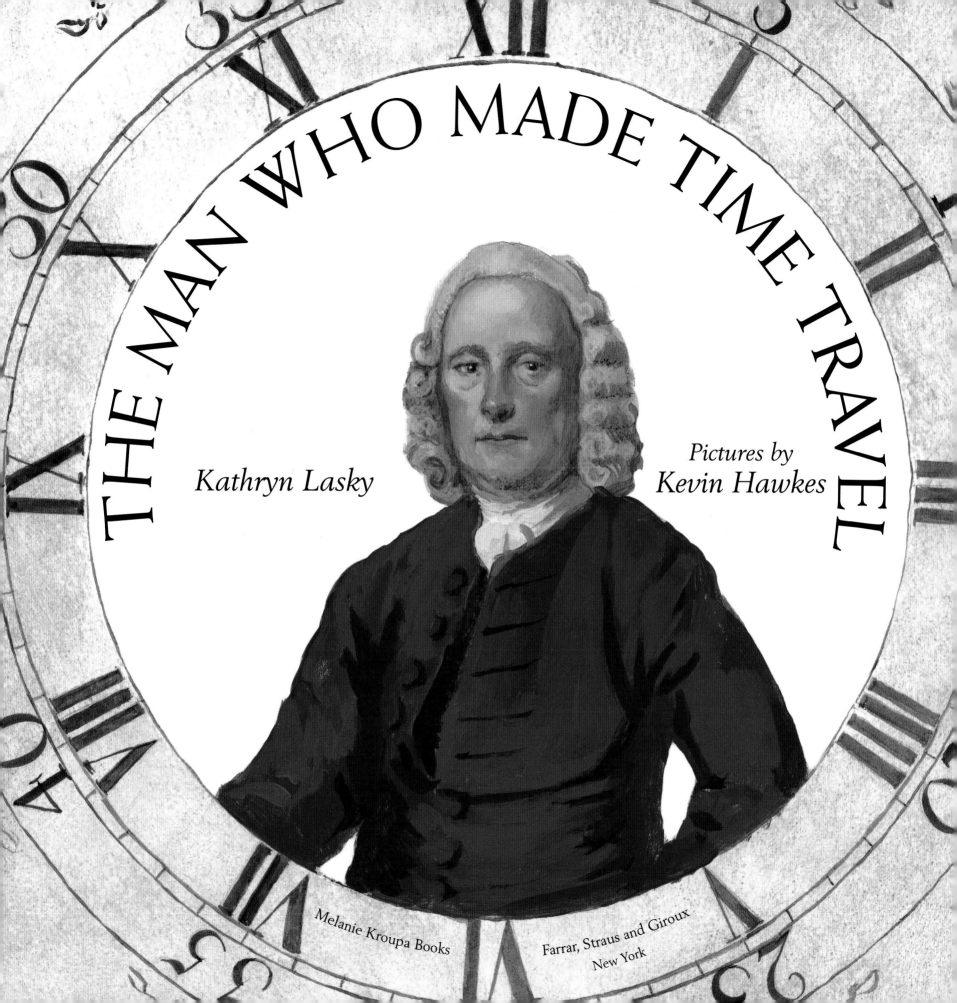

THE MAN WHO MADE TIME TRAVEL

Kathryn Lasky

Pictures by
Kevin Hawkes

Melanie Kroupa Books

Farrar, Straus and Giroux
New York

A Stormy Night

October 22, 1707

It was a mean and dirty night. The wind howled, and waves the size of small mountains crashed against the sailing ship.

Suddenly there was a sickening thud. A loud crack. The ship shuddered, then split open. It had slammed into a reef near the Scilly Isles, the outermost islands off the southwest English coast. Within minutes it sank. Moments later three other ships pierced their hulls on the same rocks.

On that foggy night nearly two thousand men died—many cursing not the land that had surprised them but the ignorance that led them onto those rocks.

The sailors died because they were lost and did not even know it. Throughout history, ships sank and men perished because there was no accurate way to measure a ship's true location.

A Matter of Time

To know a ship's position at sea, a sailor needs to know both latitude and longitude. Latitude, or the ship's north–south position, is easier to find than longitude because one can measure the height of the sun at noon or the height of the North Star above the horizon at night. This shows how far north (or south) of the equator the ship is. But to fix his location, a sailor also needs to know his east–west position—or longitude.

Longitude measurement is directly related to time. Each day, as the earth rotates, it spins eastward through the 360 degrees of a circle, moving 15 degrees each hour (15° × 24 hours = 360°). When the sun reaches its highest point overhead, it is noon local time. If this local time could be compared instantly to the time at another place, such as the home port, the distance east or west could be calculated.

If only home-port time could be bottled, it could be carried to any place on earth and compared to the local time. Then a ship's longitude could be known and the problem that had puzzled sailors for centuries would be solved.

But how *could* time be bottled? A clock set to the home-port time is the obvious answer. Unfortunately, in 1707, no clock—on land or at sea—could keep time with enough accuracy to be reliable. Precise time just couldn't travel.

If the difference between home-port and local time is 2 hours, then the difference in longitude will be 2 × 15°—or 30°—east or west of the home port.

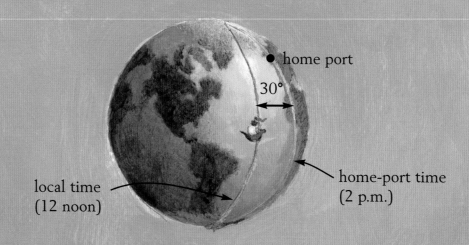

home port

30°

local time
(12 noon)

home-port time
(2 p.m.)

The Prize

The country that solved the longitude problem would rule the seas, for it could control the shipping trade, and thus gain great wealth. Seven years after the sinking of the British ships off the Scilly Isles, the British Parliament passed the Longitude Act. The act promised to pay 20,000 pounds sterling (the equivalent of at least $12 million today) for a "practicable and useful" method for measuring longitude. It created a Board of Longitude made up of scientists, mathematicians, and astronomers who would judge the entries.

And so the competition began!

God's Clock: The Lunar Distance Method

The great scientists and astronomers of the day believed there was only one answer to the longitude problem, and that answer was in the stars.

Every night the moon makes a path across the sky. On its night walk it sweeps past stars and planets. Astronomers believed that if they could accurately map the path of the moon for a year and determine the time when it passed by certain stars, they would be able to create tables sailors could use to measure their longitude. The astronomers liked the idea of this heavenly clock. It seemed predictable and reliable, even noble and divine—almost as if the starry sky at night was God's clock. Since this method of finding longitude involved measuring the apparent distance of the moon from the stars, it became known as the Lunar Distance Method.

Tiptoes and Bleeding Dogs

The most distinguished mathematicians and scientists of that time believed that the Lunar Distance Method would win the prize. But there were problems with this method. The moon is not visible every night of the month. Even when it is, measuring the distance between the moon and a star is not easy to do, particularly on the deck of a rolling ship.

There were others who were not scholars or scientists who came up with more unusual solutions. One English clergyman devised what he called the Time on Tiptoe Method. He proposed to map a row of stars and then compare them to a series of imaginary sky lines. He called this the Time on Tiptoe Method because, he foolishly reasoned, the stars moved so fast a sailor would have to run quickly on tiptoes to measure the distance between them and an imaginary sky line.

Another man claimed to have discovered a miraculous powder that could heal wounds at a distance. He suggested sending an injured dog to sea but keeping some of the dog's used bandages in the home port. Every day at a known time the healing powder would be sprinkled on the bandages. He was certain the dog on the ship would bark at the very same instant, "telling" the captain what time it was back home. But what would happen if the dog got well? Would the "barking clock" stop barking?

A man named John French invented his own preposterous solution, which involved using a brass plate with a compass needle and building a fire on deck. Not only was it dangerous (the ship could have caught fire), it had nothing to do with the measurement of longitude!

But one man had an idea that was much more sensible than bleeding dogs, running on tiptoes, or building fires, and much simpler than the lunar measurements of learned astronomers.

A Curious Boy

John Harrison was twenty-one years old when the Longitude Prize was announced. He knew full well the dangers of the sea. The village where he lived was near the bustling port of Hull.

As a boy he was one of the bell ringers in the village church of Barrow. His sense of hearing was so good that he was asked to tune the church bells. Soon he was tuning the bells of a neighboring church as well.

But bells were only John Harrison's hobby. His real work, like his father's, was carpentry. He knew wood and he knew simple mathematics. He knew these things from experience, not from a formal education.

John was curious about how things worked. When a visitor lent him a book of lectures on mathematics and Isaac Newton's laws of motion, John copied out every single word. But he also liked to figure things out for himself. So he tested Newton's basic principles of motion.

Would a heavy ball roll down a hill faster than a light ball? Does the ball gain speed as it rolls down the hill? Would the clapper in a bell swing faster if it was shorter or if it weighed more?

John Harrison proved each and every principle for himself.

From Bells to Clocks

John Harrison began to realize that bells and pendulum clocks were similar: the swinging action of the bell marked the passage of time just as the pendulum regulates the motion of a clock. He decided to build a clock. Perhaps clock building interested him because it was a way of combining his hobby, bells, with his real work, carpentry. Some people, however, snickered at the very idea of a carpenter's son making a clock.

Clocks were rare and made of valuable materials such as brass. John could not afford much brass, so he used mostly wood. The larger clock wheels he cut from oak, and the smallest gears, spindles, and axles from boxwood. He completed his first clock by the time he was twenty. Within the next four years he had built two more pendulum clocks. As his reputation grew, he was hired to build a clock in the tower of a new stable on a wealthy landowner's estate. He made a remarkable timepiece that showed the precise time from its airy perch, its wheels and gears hidden in the rafters, sharing space with roosting pigeons.

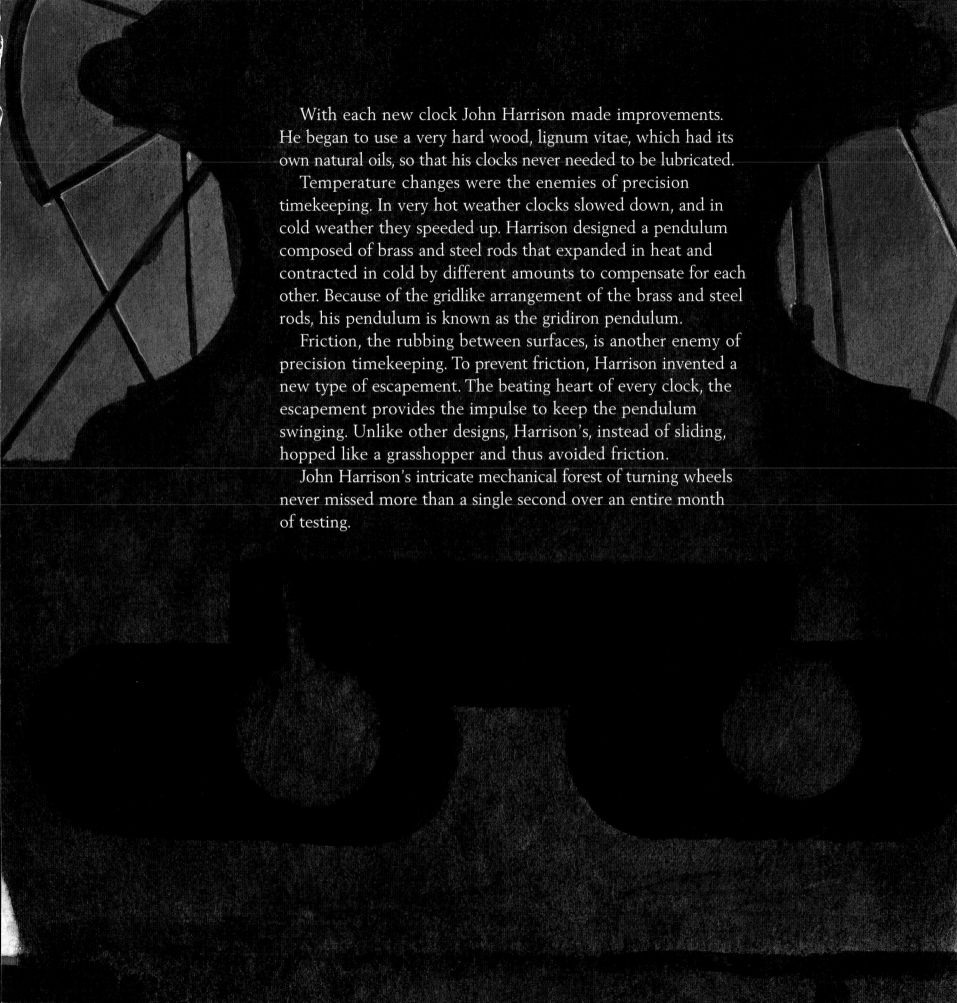

With each new clock John Harrison made improvements.
He began to use a very hard wood, lignum vitae, which had its
own natural oils, so that his clocks never needed to be lubricated.

Temperature changes were the enemies of precision
timekeeping. In very hot weather clocks slowed down, and in
cold weather they speeded up. Harrison designed a pendulum
composed of brass and steel rods that expanded in heat and
contracted in cold by different amounts to compensate for each
other. Because of the gridlike arrangement of the brass and steel
rods, his pendulum is known as the gridiron pendulum.

Friction, the rubbing between surfaces, is another enemy of
precision timekeeping. To prevent friction, Harrison invented a
new type of escapement. The beating heart of every clock, the
escapement provides the impulse to keep the pendulum
swinging. Unlike other designs, Harrison's, instead of sliding,
hopped like a grasshopper and thus avoided friction.

John Harrison's intricate mechanical forest of turning wheels
never missed more than a single second over an entire month
of testing.

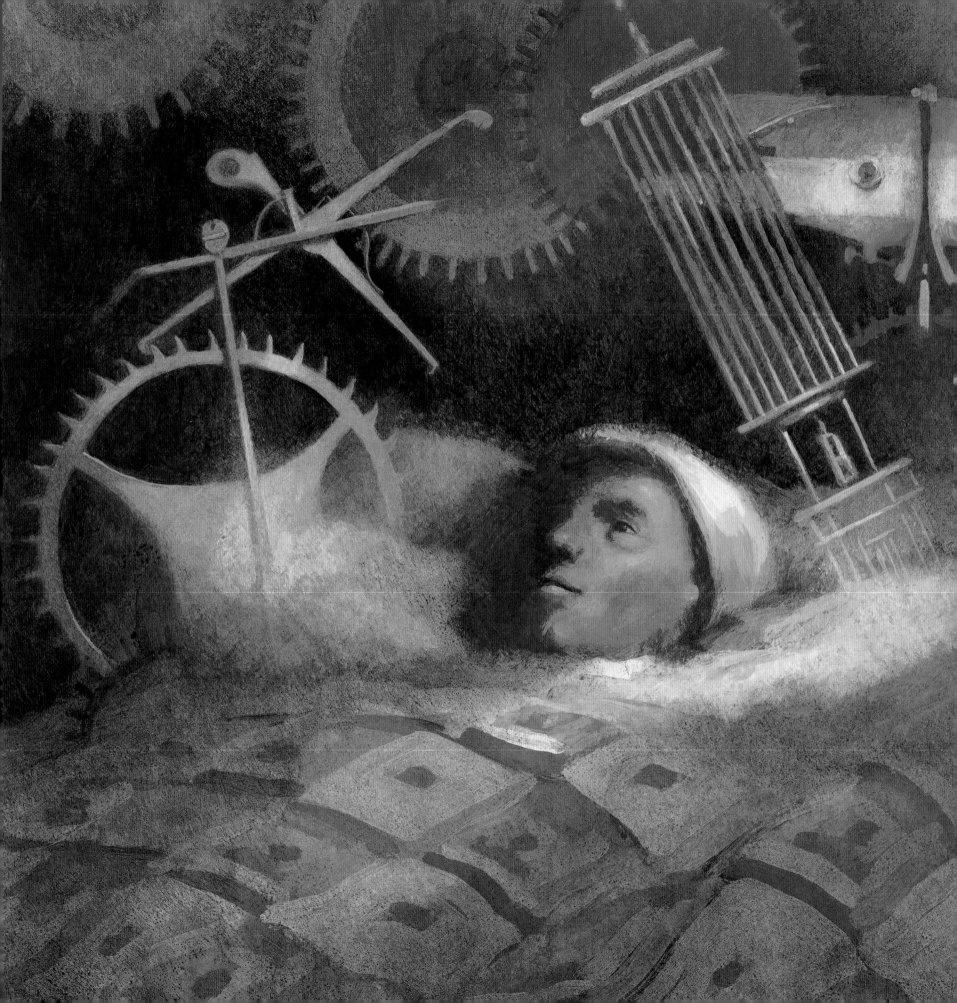

A Shipshape Clock

Like others of his generation, John Harrison puzzled over the longitude problem. He became convinced that the solution was a clock that could measure time at sea, a clock in which time could travel—travel and never lose a second because of dampness, salt air, changing temperatures, or stormy seas— a clock accurate enough to calculate longitude. Instead of using a pendulum, which wouldn't work on a rolling sea, he created seesaw balances linked—like dancing couples—by squiggly threads of steel he called worm springs. Free of gravity, they would swing evenly, no matter how rough the ocean.

Harrison dreamed of gears and spirals. He dreamed and he worked for several years on his plans. In 1730 he went to London to present his drawings and diagrams to the Board of Longitude, the group in charge of awarding the prize. He hoped it would give him enough money to build his clock.

When he arrived in London, however, the Board seemed to have vanished. Still determined, he sought out Sir Edmund Halley, the Astronomer Royal at the Greenwich Observatory. Halley was impressed by his drawings and sent him to see George Graham, London's most famous clockmaker. Graham, too, was impressed and found enough money for him to build his sea clock. John Harrison went back to Barrow to begin work.

Five years later, after hundreds of drawings and thousands of hours of delicate cutting of wooden wheels and tooling of metal parts, John Harrison completed his first sea clock, the clock now referred to as H1.

But in 1735 when he presented it to the learned men of the Royal Society, they squinted and whispered among themselves. For H1 was like no other clock. Just over two feet tall and weighing 75 pounds, it stood bright and bristling with brass rods and strange spirals, knobs, balls, and odd little springs. The twin balances with their worm springs teeter-tottered back and forth in a rhythm not unlike that of a rolling ship. Some said the clock even looked like a ship. There were no sails and no rudder, yet it seemed ready to sail, sail on any sea.

A year later the Board arranged a trial voyage to Lisbon, Portugal, for John Harrison and his clock. Throughout the entire trip the clock lost barely a second. Harrison, however, lost his breakfast, lunch, and dinner. He spent his days hanging over the ship's rail, throwing up. He must have envied his sea clock and wished that he could have devised such seaworthy balances for his own insides.

Simply Too Simple

The sea clock had proven itself. The Board of Longitude, which had not met in over twenty years, called a meeting. The members wanted to question John Harrison and see his timepiece.

But Harrison was a perfectionist. When he met with the Board, he spoke only of the improvements that he wished to make, and requested more money for designing a new clock. The Board agreed to provide funds so he could keep working, but the members must have wondered if a man-made object, a mechanical ticking thing in a box, could really tell a captain where his ship was on the vast ocean. It seemed too simple, especially when compared to measuring by the stars. It was not the heavenly clock of the Lunar Distance Method, and John Harrison was not a university professor or a scientist. To the Board, the notion of a country clockmaker solving the longitude problem seemed almost as ridiculous as a quack with his healing powders and bleeding dog.

Another Clock

John Harrison moved to London, where he spent another two years building a second sea clock. H2 was narrower and taller, so it didn't take up as much space as H1, but it was heavier, its wheels made of brass instead of wood. Bar balances counteracted the rocking motion of a ship. And the clock worked better in varying temperatures. H2 also had a new device called a remontoire that allowed it to self-wind every few minutes. This increased its precision.

Every imaginable test was performed on H2. It was heated up, cooled down, jiggled, and shaken. And still H2 kept perfect time. Yet this second sea clock was never tried at sea. Perhaps Harrison noticed a slight flaw in the bar balance. Or maybe he observed some other tiny error anyone else would have ignored. For Harrison, only perfection was good enough. So he decided to make a third sea clock.

A Third Clock

For almost twenty years John Harrison worked, tinkered, and fiddled with H3, his third sea clock. He invented a new kind of thermostat called the bimetallic strip that allowed the clock to adjust to temperature changes. He replaced the seesaw balances with balance wheels. In every way, H3 was his most complicated clock. It had 753 different parts. But it was his smallest and lightest clock so far.

As the clockmaker meticulously fine-tuned H3, he himself was also changing. The hair beneath his wig grew thinner, his face more drawn and wrinkled. His son, William, only a baby when he had first started H1 and most likely a nuisance in Harrison's workshop, had grown into a young man in his twenties who now helped his father on this clock, H3.

Although H3 was sleek and beautiful, like H2 it was never tested at sea. It also did not keep time as accurately as John Harrison had hoped. In fact, he was so disappointed that even after all his years of work, he felt that he must invent a completely *new* timepiece.

Running Out of Time

For John Harrison himself time was becoming a problem—it was running out. At sixty, he was tired from his work on H3 but not too tired to design a new pocket watch for himself. Not having the skills of a watchmaker, he asked a fellow clockmaker, John Jefferys, to build it for him.

It was a perfect little watch, and he admired it greatly. And then he had an idea. Could a pocket watch be made accurate enough for use on a ship? The more John Harrison considered this possibility, the more sense it made.

He began working on his new timepiece in 1755. When he finished, H4 measured five inches across—only slightly larger than a typical pocket watch—and weighed only three pounds. Its calm white face was encased in two dazzling silver shells decorated with fruits and leaves. Beneath this face was a miniature world of spinning wheels and tiny cut jewels, diamonds and rubies, that made all the parts turn smoothly.

In 1760 John Harrison asked the Board of Longitude for a sea trial for H4. They agreed. Soon John's son, William, was on a ship bound for Jamaica. On the return trip the weather was so stormy that he had to wrap up H4 in blankets and hold it like a newborn to protect it from the raging seas. But still it ticked on. After 147 days at sea, H4's error was only one minute and 54 seconds, a remarkable achievement for any clock in an era when even a timepiece on solid land might have errors of several minutes.

An Enemy of Clocks

It had been nearly fifty years since the Longitude Act had been passed and the prize offered. H4 should have won the moment William returned to England. Every requirement had been met, but suddenly H4's reliability was questioned. Was the trial a fluke? Could its performance be repeated? New tests were ordered for H4. One member of the Board of Longitude was chiefly responsible for these tests. His name was Nevil Maskelyne.

Nevil Maskelyne believed absolutely in the Lunar Distance Method. As Astronomer Royal, he insisted it was the only practical solution to the longitude problem. He thought ticking things in boxes were untrustworthy and pocket watches that solved mathematical and astronomical problems unbelievable. Even though H4 had passed the new tests with flying colors, Maskelyne called John Harrison a "mere mechanic." He would move H4 and Harrison's other timepieces to the Royal Observatory at Greenwich. There he would test them himself.

It must have been painful for John Harrison to watch Nevil Maskelyne cart away the clocks that had ticked quietly in his workshop for thirty years. He returned to his private room, only to suddenly hear a terrible crash. H1 lay shattered! One of Maskelyne's workers had dropped it.

Under Maskelyne's critical eyes, H4, which had gone through two sea voyages while losing less than two minutes, failed its tests miserably. But the testing conditions were far from ideal. Not only was H4 housed in direct sunlight, where it endured stifling heat, it was monitored by elderly retired seamen who were so feeble they could barely climb the hill to the Royal Observatory. Maskelyne announced to the world that "the watch could not be trusted." So the Board ordered John Harrison to make yet another timepiece.

The Clockmaker and the King

H5 was very plain. There were no leaves or flowers on its dial as there had been with H4. Nearing his seventy-ninth birthday, perhaps John Harrison felt he did not have the time for such decorations. His eyesight was failing. He was bothered by gout.

The clock met every single requirement of the Longitude Act, but still the Board would not give him the prize. How much time did such an old man have left? There was only one thing to do: petition the King.

So he did. In January 1772, his son William presented their case to King George III. "These people have been cruelly treated," the King reportedly whispered after William finished recounting their history. Then he is said to have exclaimed, "By God, Harrison, I will see you righted!"

A trial was arranged for H5 in the King's quarters. At first the watch behaved strangely. Then it was discovered that in a nearby closet there were magnetic rocks, called lodestones, that affected the metallic parts of the clock. As soon as the lodestones were removed, H5 performed perfectly.

Finally, on June 21, 1773, an Act of Parliament awarded John Harrison the remaining prize money he deserved. Even so, the Board of Longitude *still* refused to name him as the official prizewinner. In fact, the long-sought-after Longitude Prize was never officially awarded to anyone.

A Timeless Hero

Time traveled very well in John Harrison's clocks. Because of them, great explorers such as Captain James Cook were able to find their longitude on all the oceans of the world. Harrison became the hero not only of clockmakers but of dreamers and ordinary people everywhere who learned by doing and daring. For it was not the heavenly clock of the university astronomers, with their blind faith in the stars, which allowed Britain to rule the seas and eventually led to the creation of the British Empire. Instead it was a clock made by a man—a man from the rough north country, a man who had never attended the grand universities, a bell ringer, a man who knew wood, the laws of motion, and how to tune a bell, a carpenter, an inventor, and, most of all, a clockmaker.

H1, H2, H3, and H4 are currently on display at the National Maritime Museum in Greenwich, England. H5 can be seen at the Clockmakers' Museum in Guildhall, London.

H5
Similar to H4, but without decorations
Completed in 1772—Harrison age 79

H4
5 inches across, weighs 3 pounds
Looks like a large, beautifully decorated
  pocket watch
Uses jewels as bearings to reduce friction
Completed in 1759—Harrison age 66

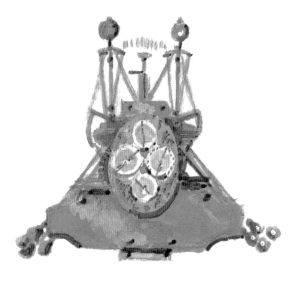

H1
25 inches tall, weighs 75 pounds
Wheels made of wood
Introduces seesaw balances with worm springs
Completed in 1735—Harrison age 42

H2
26 inches tall, weighs 86 pounds
Wheels made of brass
Introduces a new kind of remontoire
*   (a device to keep the clock running*
*   during rewinding)*
Completed in 1739—Harrison age 46

H3
23 inches tall, weighs 60 pounds, 753 separate parts
*   (takes up less than a third the space of H1)*
Replaces balance bars with circular balances linked
*   by metal ribbons*
Introduces the bimetallic strip and the caged roller
*   bearing (forerunner of today's ball bearing)*
Completed in 1757—Harrison age 64

Author's Note and Acknowledgments

Almost thirty years ago my husband, Christopher Knight, and I made a transatlantic crossing in a small ketch-rigged sailboat. At that time Global Positioning System satellites were not available to civilians. We navigated across the Atlantic Ocean—Boston, Massachusetts, to Falmouth, England—by the sun and stars, using only a sextant and a chronometer. But it worked. Our sun sights were precise enough; our chronometer never slipped more than a fraction of a second. We found our way to England and back.

What was unimaginable to me was that sailors as recently as the early eighteenth century did not have any comparable means of navigation. Because of their inability to know longitude, they could be lost as soon as they were away from the sight of land.

It was a month after we got to England that we visited the National Maritime Museum in Greenwich and I viewed for the first time John Harrison's wonderful timekeepers, now called chronometers. With the exception of H4, they were massive compared to the small chronometer aboard our boat, yet I knew they did the same job. For some reason I found a profound joy and satisfaction in this; a feeling of historical continuity with the age of great navigation and sailing exploration by heroes such as Captain James Cook.

Many years later, when I decided to do a book about John Harrison, my husband and I returned to England (by plane, not boat) and spent several days at Greenwich examining these same beautiful, complicated timepieces. I am forever indebted to William J. H. Andrewes, the former David P. Wheatland Curator of the Collection of Historical Scientific Instruments at Harvard University, editor of *The Quest for Longitude*, and co-author of *The Illustrated Longitude*, for his careful reading of this manuscript and his patient explanations. I would also like to thank Jonathan Betts, Keeper of Horology at the National Maritime Museum in Greenwich, for the time he generously spent explaining the mechanical principles and physics of Harrison's chronometers, H1, H2, H3, H4, and H5. In addition, my husband and I traveled to Brocklesby Park in Lincolnshire and visited the estate of the Earl of Yarborough, where one of Harrison's wooden clocks still ticks in the tower of the stable. We are very grateful to Mr. Raymond, keeper of the clock, for explaining its mechanism, which has been maintaining excellent time for 280 years.

This book represented an enormous challenge for me, as mathematics and physics are not my strength. I am indebted to my husband for helping me understand, with countless diagrams and patient explanations, many difficult concepts.

Finally, I must say something about John Harrison himself. What puts me in awe of this man is his persistence, his total dedication to his work. He found in it a nobility that needed no prizes. To me that is the sign of true genius.

—K.L.

Bibliography

Kathryn Lasky:

Andrewes, William, J. H., ed. *The Quest for Longitude*. Cambridge, Mass.: Collection of Historical Scientific Instruments, Harvard University, 1996.

Betts, Jonathan. *John Harrison*. London: National Maritime Museum, 1993.

Coleman, Satis N. *Bells: Their History, Legends, Making and Uses*. New York: Rand McNally, 1971.

Ellacombe, Henry Thomas. *Practical Remarks on Belfries and Ringers*. London: Bell and Daldy, 1860–61.

Landes, David S. *Revolution in Time*. Cambridge, Mass.: Harvard University Press, 1983.

Lankford, John, ed. *History of Astronomy: An Encyclopedia*. New York: Garland, 1997.

Macey, Samuel L., ed. *Encyclopedia of Time*. New York: Garland, 1994.

Peinkofer, Karl, and Fritz Tannigel. *Handbook of Percussion Instruments*. New York: Schott, 1969.

Sobel, Dava. *Longitude*. New York: Walker, 1995.

Sobel, Dava, and William J. H. Andrewes. *The Illustrated Longitude*. New York: Walker, 1998.

Taylor, Henry W. *The Art and Science of the Timpani*. London: John Baker, 1964.

Tufts, Nancy Poore. *The Art of Handbell Ringing*. New York: Abingdon Press, 1961.

Kevin Hawkes:

Andrewes, William J. H., ed. *The Quest for Longitude*. Cambridge, Mass.: Collection of Historical Scientific Instruments, Harvard University, 1996.

Hansen, H. J. *Art and the Sea Farer*. New York: Viking Press, 1968.

Lippincott, Kristen. *A Guide to the Old Royal Observatory: The Story of Time and Space*. Greenwich, England: The National Maritime Museum, [n. d.].

Nicolson, Benedict. *Joseph Wright of Derby, Painter of Light*. New Haven: Yale University Press, 1971.

Paulson, Ronald. *Hogarth: His Life, Art and Times*. New Haven: Yale University Press, 1971.

Quill, Humphrey. *John Harrison*. London: John Baker, 1966.

Sobel, Dava, and William J. H. Andrewes. *The Illustrated Longitude*. New York: Walker, 1998.

For Chris, who gets me there
—K.L.

For Larry, Robin, Sarah, and Nathaniel

And with many thanks to Will Andrewes for his thoughtful comments and suggestions and to Kathryn Lasky and Christopher Knight for their on-site photographs and reference material
—K.H.

Illustration Notes

Endpapers: pictured is Harrison's revolutionary watch, H4, face (left), back plate (right)

This page and facing page: The four designs within the border are those Harrison considered for H4. He selected the design that appears at the bottom.

Text copyright © 2003 by Kathryn Lasky
Illustrations copyright © 2003 by Kevin Hawkes
All rights reserved
Distributed in Canada by Douglas & McIntyre Ltd.
Color separations by Bright Arts (HK) Ltd
Printed and bound in Hong Kong by South China Printing Company Limited
Designed by Jennifer Browne
First edition, 2003
10 9 8 7 6 5 4 3 2

Library of Congress Cataloging-in-Publication Data
Lasky, Kathryn.
    The man who made time travel / Kathryn Lasky ; paintings by Kevin Hawkes.
        p. cm.
    Summary: Describes the need for sailors to be able to determine their position at sea and the efforts of John Harrison, an eighteenth century man who spent his life refining instruments to enable them to do this.
    ISBN 0-374-34788-3
    1. Chronometers—History—Juvenile literature.   2. Longitude—Measurement—History—Juvenile literature.   3. Harrison, John, 1693–1776—Juvenile literature.   4. Clock and watch makers—Great Britain—Biography—Juvenile literature.   [1. Longitude—Measurement.   2. Harrison, John, 1693–1776.   3. Chronometers.]   I. Hawkes, Kevin, ill. II. Title.

QB107 .L37 2002
526'.62'09—dc21
                                                        2001033266